SEWING MACHINE

MAGIC

MAKE THE MOST OF YOUR MACHINE

- Demystify Presser Feet and Other Accessories
- Tips and Tricks for Smooth Sewing
- 10 Easy, Creative Projects

STEFFANI LINCECUM

Creative Publishing international

Inspiring | Educating | Creating | Entertaining

Brimming with creative inspiration, how-to projects, and useful information to enrich your everyday life, Quarto Knows is a favorite destination for those pursuing their interests and passions. Visit our site and dig deeper with our books into your area of interest: Quarto Creates, Quarto Cooks, Quarto Homes, Quarto Lives, Quarto Drives, Quarto Explores, Quarto Gifts, or Quarto Kids.

First published in 2017 by Creative Publishing international, an imprint of The Quarto Group,
401 Second Avenue North, Suite 310, Minneapolis, MN 55401, USA.
T (612) 344-8100 F (612) 344-8692 QuartoKnows.com

Creative Publishing international titles are also available at discount for retail, wholesale, promotional, and bulk purchase. For details, contact the Special Sales Manager by email at specialsales@quarto.com or by mail at The Quarto Group, Attn: Special Sales Manager, 401 Second Avenue North, Suite 310, Minneapolis, MN 55401, USA.

10 9 8 7 6 5 4 3 2 1

ISBN: 978-1-58923-950-0

Digital edition published in 2017
eISBN: 978-1-63159-442-7

Library of Congress Cataloging-in-Publication Data available

Cover and Book Design: Megan Jones Design
Photography: Timothy Hughes Photographics
Illustration: Steffani Lincecum

Printed in China

In memory of Ezma Schoemann (1920–1990).

CONTENTS

5

PRESSER FEET FOR CREATIVITY

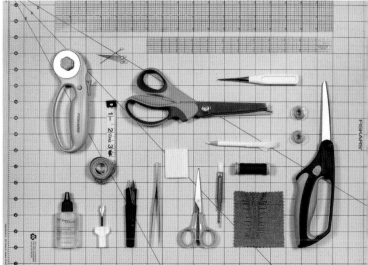

PREFACE

My husband and I call sewing classes "magic shows." We started saying this after I told him about getting oohs and aahs of revelation from students, as if I'm performing some sleight of hand. I felt that same way when I took a sewing class from Natalie "Alabama" Chanin and she enthralled the group with her demonstration of the physics of sewing and taught us all about "loving our thread." What seems like magic, and sleight of hand, is actually knowledge of how the machine works and, of course, practice.

I have learned in more than thirty years of professional sewing that the keys to success are the right tools and plenty of practice. I started my sewing career with the very basic knowledge of how to thread a machine and wind a bobbin, eventually making everything from costumes to curtains. There was a mystery box of items that came with the machine, and some other items I got from my grandmother, but in the beginning, I used only the basic foot that came on the machine. I learned from zipper package instructions how to use the zipper foot and even figured out that you could use it to install piping!

But do you know that feeling you get when you've lost your sewing mojo? Do you get frustrated when everything's going fine, but suddenly your machine decides to jam or make thread nests under your fabric? So, you rethread, and the same thing happens, rethread again, and the machine works. What the heck happened? Well, I learned after trial and error, reading my manual, and taking lessons that all these problems were fixable and—better yet—avoidable, if I just understood how the machine worked.

With *Sewing Machine Magic*, I give you the distillation of all my research, trials, and errors! No matter how long you've been sewing, you'll find information, tips, and guidelines in this book to help you enjoy a smoother sewing experience. Your sewing mojo is right here. Make some magic!

Baby Blanket (see page 105)

FINDING THE RIGHT MACHINE

All sewing machines do the same thing: they join layers of fabric together by inserting threads between them. As you explore different kinds of machines, you'll find that most machines add a variety of unique features to this basic function. The key to determining the best machine for you is knowing which of these extra features you need or want.

Just like other appliances and even cars, there are many manufacturers that sell several types of sewing machines. Every brand usually sells all levels of machines, from entry level and less expensive basic machines, to intermediate machines with more features, to high-end machines that are more expensive, with more elaborate features.

Different brands are known for different things, and you're bound to hear lots of opinions when you start researching. Choose the brand that feels right when you take it for a "test drive." And, be sure to purchase your machine from a friendly, helpful sewing shop—one that is available if you run into problems, offers classes, and, of course, provides general maintenance. Because you'll probably find your favorite brand, let's, for our purposes, assume that all brands are equal and just look at the various features you'll want to consider.

Types of Sewing Machines

There are three main types: mechanical, electronic, and computerized. There are also machines with features designed specifically for decorative sewing and quilting enthusiasts.

Mechanical machines are the basic workhorses of the sewing world. They perform the functions that the average sewist needs and are usually the most affordable. You choose different sewing functions on these machines by moving mechanical levers and dials. On some mechanical models, you can move the needle position to the left or right, in varying degrees. You can also make manual buttonholes on most models, but you'll need to mark the size of the buttonhole on the fabric and then move the stitch dial to form the buttonhole.

Electronic machines fall in the middle of the field, both in price point and in number of special features. Some features include the ability of the machine to stop in a "needle up" or "needle down" position and to adjust the needle position in small increments for really precise sewing. Electronic machines have more decorative stitches than mechanical machines do, including stitches that are programmed and stored in the machine's memory. They can also stitch small letters and numbers in a line of decorative stitching, combine decorative stitches, and store those sequences. They also have a selection of automatic buttonholes, requiring no manual adjustments. These are great features to have, especially if you're doing a lot of garment sewing where you need precise needle position for topstitching or needle-down position for accurate corners and curves like those in shirt making and tailoring. Controlling stitch length and width, stitch selection, and even changes in tension settings are done by interacting with buttons or directly on a small screen, instead of with mechanical dials and levers.

Computerized machines, also called embroidery machines, are the top of the line. They have all the utility stitches, decorative stitches, memory capacity, and needle-position features of the mechanical and electronic machines, but the computer in these machines allows the user to stitch very complex embroidery designs. They can be programmed to stitch letters and numbers, as well as monograms and words much larger in scale than those stitched on electronic machines. These designs are stored in the machine's memory or can be downloaded from another computer or stored on a USB stick.

Computerized machines with advanced embroidery capabilities are compatible with separate embroidery design software that allows you to create your own designs. They come with various hoops that hold your work in place and usually a separate embroidery unit with an arm that moves the hoop back and forth while the needle works in decorative and zigzag patterns to create the designs. These designs can be much larger than the single rows (up to ⅓" [8.5 mm] wide) of stitching you get with an electronic machine. Some computerized machines have feeding mechanisms that not only feed forward and backward but also sideways, allowing what are called Maxi Stitch patterns up to 2" (52 mm) wide!

Any of these machines can be used for quilting, garment sewing, tailoring, and repairs. Some are designed specifically for quilters and have unique features, such as a larger space between the needle and the upright part of the machine (called harp space) to maneuver large, bulky projects. They also have stitches that replicate hand stitching and come with accessories such as free motion feet (see page 118).

Characteristics of Sewing Machines

MECHANICAL MACHINES

- Most affordable
- Most utility stitches
- Some stretch stitches
- Limited decorative stitches
- Multistep, manual buttonhole
- Levers or dials for needle position, stitch width, stitch length

ELECTRONIC MACHINES

- Middle price range
- Range of utility stitches
- Range of stretch stitches
- Linear decorative stitches
- One-step, automatic buttonholes (variety of styles)
- LCD screen and/or push-button control for needle position, stitch width, stitch length
- Needle-down position
- Speed control

COMPUTERIZED AND COMPUTERIZED SEWING/EMBROIDERY MACHINES

- Upper price range
- Large range of utility stitches
- Large range of stretch stitches
- Large variety of linear and hooped decorative stitches
- One-step, automatic buttonhole (variety of styles)
- LCD screen control for stitch selection, width, and length
- Needle up/down position
- Speed control
- Embroidery capabilities
- Detachable embroidery units that can be removed for regular sewing
- Interaction with other computers or USB drives
- Some have side-to-side feed for Maxi Stitches without a hoop

COMPUTERIZED EMBROIDERY-ONLY MACHINES

- Used only to stitch embroidery designs
- Interacts with computer software or memory sticks to load designs
- Dedicated to embroidery without other regular sewing features

QUILTING MACHINES

- Electronic machines with larger harp space
- Quilter-friendly features, heirloom stitches, and appliqué stitches
- Specialty feet, such as open-toe foot, free motion foot, and ¼" (6 mm) guide foot
- Some have a hands-free knee lifter to raise the presser foot

FINDING YOUR SEWING PERSONALITY

Mechanical Machine: I just want a reliable, simple to understand machine. I know I can always get extra accessories, as I need them. If I need to make a buttonhole, I can, but I don't really plan on making a lot of them.

Electronic Machine: I love to sew and I want a reliable machine with a lot of features. I want to be able to choose from a selection of one-step buttonholes, and I want the machine to stitch them without me having to control every step. I'd like to be able to stitch with great precision; stopping the needle in the down position for corners and curves is important to me. I also like having a large assortment of utility and decorative stitch choices, but I don't really care to embroider large projects in a hoop.

Quilting Machine: I'm a quilter, and I like having just the right tool for the job! I love making large projects, and I enjoy using techniques like appliqué and free motion quilting, heirloom stitches like blanket stitch, featherstitch, and candle-wicking stitches.

Computerized Sewing and Embroidery Machine: I know I want the flexibility to make whatever I can dream up and not be limited by my machine. I want to stitch garments, home décor, and accessories and then embellish them with decorative stitches and large embroidery. I want to know that I have the ability to do that without the need for two different machines. It's exciting to think about downloading designs and making something truly unique. I like knowing that I have all the bells and whistles!

Embroidery-Only Machine: I just want to embellish and decorate! I have no desire to cut and sew a garment or a bag; just let me embellish one that's already made. I like the idea of embroidering gifts for friends and family or maybe even starting a small embroidery business. I probably already have another sewing machine that I'm really happy with, so I just need one that does large-hooped embroidery.

NO

Do you want a large selection of stitches and the maximum ability to control the left to right needle position and whether it stops in an up or down position?

NO

MECHANICAL:
- Most affordable
- Utility stitches
- Stretch stitches
- Decorative stitches
- Multistep buttonhole
- Push buttons or dials for needle position, stitch width, and stitch length

I just want a reliable, simple to understand machine. I know I can always get extra accessories as I need them. If I need to make a buttonhole, I can, but I don't really plan on needing to making a lot of them.

NO

ELECTRONIC:
- Middle price range
- Utility stitches
- Stretch stitches
- Decorative stitches
- One-step buttonhole
- LCD screen and/or push button control for needle position, stitch width, and stitch length
- Needle down position
- Speed control

I want a reliable machine with a lot of features. I want to be able to choose from a selection of one-step buttonholes and like to be able to stitch with great precision. Stopping the needle in a down position for corners and curves is important to me. I like knowing that I have lots of choices of both utility and decorative stitches, but I don't really care to embroider large projects in a hoop.

Which Machine Suits You?

START HERE

Do you want be able to do embroidery projects?

YES

Do you want to be able to sew entire garments, bags, or projects?

NO

YES

YES

Do you plan on doing a lot of quilting? Do you want a large selection of heirloom stitches, quilting-specific features, and extra space for large projects?

YES

QUILTING MACHINES:
- Electronic machines with larger harp space
- Quilter-friendly features such as heirlook stitches and applique stitches
- Specialty feet with quilting in mind such as open toe, free motion, and ¼" (6 mm) guide foot

I'm a quilter, and I like having just the right tool for the job! I love making large projects, and enjoy using techniques like appliqué and free motion quilting.

EMBROIDERY ONLY:
- Used only to stitch out embroidery designs
- Interact with computer or memory sticks to load designs
- Dedicated to embroidery without other regular sewing features

I just want to create! I have no desire to cut and sew a garment or a bag, just let me embellish one that's already made!

COMPUTERIZED UPPER PRICE RANGE
- Utility stitches
- Stretch stitches
- Decorative stitches
- One-step buttonhole
- Screen for stitch selection, width, length, needle up/down position
- Speed control
- Optional embroidery capabilities
- Detachable embroidery units
- Interaction with other computers or USB drives, side-to-side feed for maxi stitches without a hoop on some

I know I want the flexibility to make whatever I can dream up and not be limited by my machine. I want to make and embellish and know that I have the ability to do that without having two different machines for making and creating. It's exciting to think about downloading designs and making something truly unique. I like knowing that I have all the bells and whistles!

ABOUT PRESSER FEET

Because this book is about to open up the magic of presser feet for you, you'll want to know which kind your machine uses, how they attach to your machine, and where to find them. The good news is that you can find presser feet or adaptors for every sewing machine brand, and you'll probably want them all (eventually)!

Presser feet are first described by how they attach to the sewing machine and then by the function they perform (covered in the following chapters). All feet fall into the following attachment categories: high shank, low shank, slant shank, snap-on, or Bernina feet. The shank is the upright portion of the foot that attaches to the presser foot bar.

Nevertheless, it is possible to use generic snap-on feet if you use a snap-on adaptor designed for your machine. For more information, see "Presser Foot Adaptors" on page 15.

High shank, low shank, and slant shank feet require a screwdriver for attachment and removal from the machine. The screwdriver comes with the machine. Be sure to tighten the screw securely so the foot doesn't come loose and interfere with the needle. I've broken more than a few needles because I didn't tighten that screw enough.

The first thing you'll need to know before shopping for presser feet is the type of shank your sewing machine requires. Check your sewing machine manual or your local dealer to confirm what type of feet fit your machine. Even within brands, some feet are not interchangeable due to the width of the feed teeth and the opening needed for the needle. Some newer computerized machines have extra-wide stitches and need feet designed for that larger clearance. It's always good to do a little research.

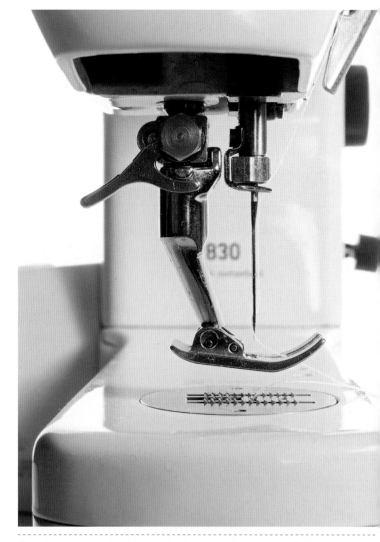

Bernina presser feet have their own unique way of attaching to the machine and they aren't interchangeable with presser feet from other brands. Even among Bernina feet, there are three types of attachments for various generations of machines.

SNAP ON

LOW SHANK

HIGH SHANK

SLANT SHANK

BERNINA

Slant shank feet are found only on Singer machines from the 1960s and '70s.

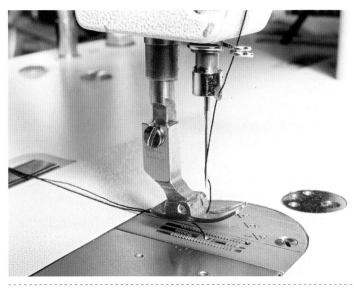

High shank feet are typically used on industrial machines and older model (pre-1980s) domestic machines. Super high shank feet are found on some vintage Kenmores and they look like slant shanks on steroids!

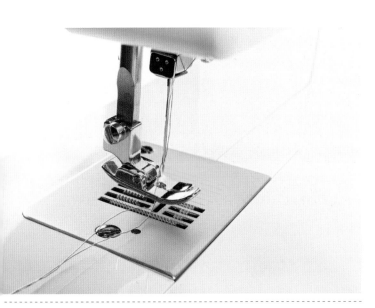

Low shank feet are common on most contemporary mechanical machines.

Snap-on feet are the easiest to use and, since the 1980s, they have become the most common type of presser feet. They snap on and off a bar on the foot holder; some have a lever or a button to release the foot once it's on, and others just snap off by pulling down on the foot.

FINDING FEET

People are often surprised to learn that each type of presser foot we cover in this book is available for any sewing machine. However, there are specific ones designed explicitly for your type of machine. Go to your nearest sewing machine repair shop and give them the brand and model number of your machine and they'll have the foot in stock for your machine or will be able to order it.

You can also search online. Be sure to include the name of the presser foot or accessory and the brand and model number of your machine in the search. You'll be amazed at all the resources available for your machine! This is also how you can find an instruction manual for your machine if you no longer have it.

 TIP: The instructions in this book are general instructions for most machines, but all machines are a bit different. Always defer to your owner's manual if you are in doubt about any of the information provided in the following chapters.

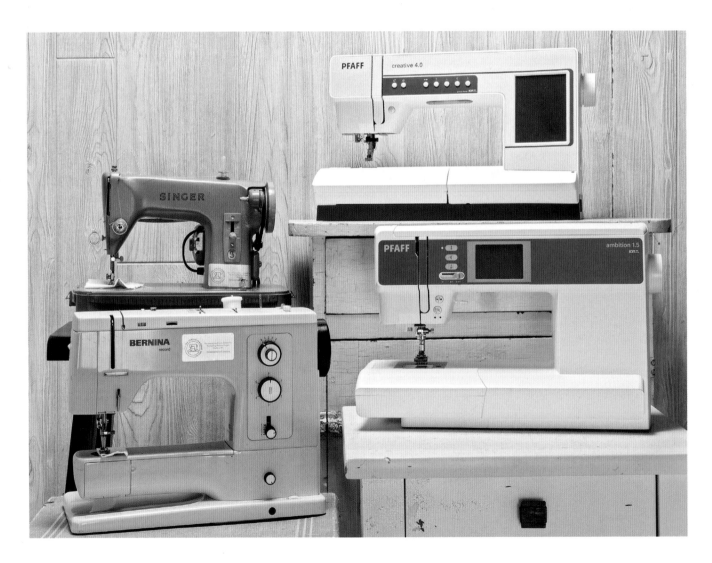

Presser Feet Adaptors

Most machines can accommodate generic snap-on feet with an adaptor. A slant shank machine requires a slant shank snap-on adaptor, a low shank machine uses a low foot snap-on adaptor, and so on. The adaptor attaches to the shank of the machine with a screwdriver so you can use snap-on feet and not have to unscrew the foot from the shank every time you want to change feet. Pretty cool! You still need to check that the needle opening in the foot is wide enough for your machine. Make sure you include your machine's model in any search for an adaptor.

A selection of shank adaptors from left to right: low shank to snap-on for a Pfaff; low shank to snap-on for most brands (generic); high shank to snap-on for most brands (generic); slant shank to snap-on for most brands (generic); Bernina to low shank.

1

TIPS
FOR SMOOTH SEWING

This book could have been called _How to Sew More and Scream Less._ When you first learn to sew and create, it can be both exhilarating and frustrating. You might have started your sewing adventure on a machine that had already been threaded by someone else or you might have had someone available to help you with obstacles, but there always comes a time when you're on your own working on a project and nothing seems to go right. Some people stop at this point because it's no fun when you're flustered and disappointed by the process.

Linen Napkins with Decorative Stitching (see page 137)

I had been sewing for many years when I found myself on a wardrobe trailer in the middle of nowhere shooting a movie. There was no one to ask when something went wrong with the machine, so I started reading the manual. The simple act of looking at the diagrams and how the machine worked was a big turning point for me, and it was certainly instrumental in making sewing more fun. After reading the manual, I knew exactly how to thread my bobbin and how important it was to do it correctly. I also learned what all the strange gadgets that came with the machine did. Over the years, I've picked up so many tips and tricks that make sewing more efficient and easy. These techniques, shared in this book, will help you sew with a smooth and steady hand instead of a halting workflow in which you might "unsew" more than you actually sew.

This chapter covers features that are universal to all machines, no matter the brand or the cost. It explains how to thread the machine, why the threading order is important, and the significance of each part of the sewing machine. It introduces many of the accessories that I've found to be helpful in providing a better sewing experience. Additionally, you'll learn about factors like fabric choice and stabilizing materials. Read on for smooth sewing and great-looking projects, no matter which machine you use!

THREAD MANAGEMENT

The main goal of a sewing machine is to deliver thread to precise locations between pieces of fabric (or other materials), with the purpose of joining those pieces. The machine must deliver just enough thread, but not too much, at just the right time and at the exact location. This means that there are many variables that affect the delivery of the thread. Learning about the thread path can help you troubleshoot when stitching goes awry. It's time to learn the correct way to thread all sewing machines.

Thread Path

The threading direction, from the spool pin to the needle, is called the thread path. Your machine's thread path is illustrated in your manual and often on the body of the sewing machine. All machines have certain features on the thread path that are the same, including a spool pin, thread guides, tension disks, a take-up lever, and a needle.

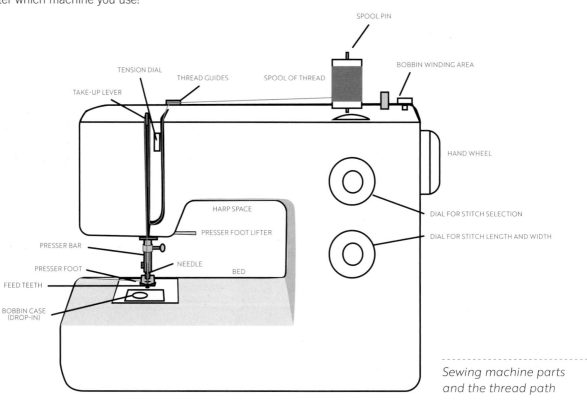

Sewing machine parts and the thread path

Spool caps

Felt pad

The **spool pin** holds the thread. Sometimes, the thread comes off the top of the machine vertically, and sometimes the spool pins are positioned so the thread can be released both vertically and horizontally.

The **spool caps** hold the thread spool on the spool pin and keep the thread from snagging on the spool. They come in various sizes. It's best to use the size spool cap that facilitates the flow of the thread. For a narrow spool of thread, use the smallest spool cap. If you have a wider spool, use the wider cap, which directs the thread past the rough edges of the spool and around the smooth spool cap.

 TIP: Not all vintage machines have spool caps, but you might be able to use spool caps from newer models.

Felt pads are small pads of felt that sit on the base of the spool pin. Without these pads, the spool spins too fast, releasing too much thread, causing the thread to tangle around the underside of the spool.

Thread guides are designed to control the speed of the thread's delivery and keep it from catching on something when the thread is slack. As thread comes off the spool, there are guides across the top and down the front of the machine that help keep the thread in the thread path. Check the owner's manual for locating your machine's thread guides.

Tension disks regulate the speed your thread feeds into the sewing area. *It is very important that the presser foot is raised* when you thread the machine; the raised presser foot ensures that the tension disks are open and the thread

can slide between them. There is a dial on the machine for adjusting the thread tension to accommodate fabric type and stitching applications. See page 21 for more about the tension disks.

The **take-up lever** maintains tension on the thread as it feeds into the needle. Once the thread has passed through the tension disks, it is threaded into the take-up lever (or uptake lever). Note that when the needle is in its uppermost position, the take-up lever is also in its uppermost position and vise versa. From the take-up lever, the thread goes through a thread guide as it moves toward the needle. Always make sure you are threading the machine from the side of the spool pin toward the side with the needle.

 TIP: If you don't see the take-up lever, turn the hand wheel toward you slowly until you see the silver bar with the hole emerge from the upper edge of the machine above the needle.

The **needle** delivers the upper thread layers between the layers of the fabrics, where it joins the bobbin thread (see page 28). Insert the needle into the machine and then thread the needle according to the owner's manual. The needle is usually threaded from front to back on newer machines and from left to right on some vintage or industrial machines.

How to Pull Up the Bobbin Thread

1. To retrieve the bobbin thread, hold onto the needle thread and turn the hand wheel, located on the right side of the machine, toward you. This moves the bobbin hook (under the throat plate) so it catches the upper thread.

2. Pull the upper thread gently and the bobbin thread will come up through the throat plate into the sewing area.

3. Pull both the needle and bobbin threads behind the presser foot toward the back of the machine ("parking your threads") so there are tails to hold as you begin to sew.

The Connection Between Tension Disks and Presser Feet

Here's one of those magical nuggets that will change the way you think about your machine. The tension disks, which on a modern machine are concealed but on vintage machines are visible (see photo at right), are directly connected to the presser foot. Using a vintage machine as an example so you can see the mechanism clearly, when the presser foot is down and you are sewing, the tension disks are closed (A) and the amount of pressure applied by the presser foot keeps the thread flowing steadily to the needle. When the presser foot is lifted and you aren't sewing, the disks are open (B) and you're able to pull the work out smoothly from the machine. If the thread doesn't pull out smoothly, make sure you've finished your stitch by rolling the hand wheel toward you and stopping with the needle in the uppermost position.

A very common mistake is threading the machine with the presser foot down. This closes the tension disks and doesn't allow the thread to be seated between the disks properly.

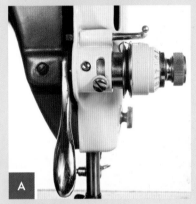

Another common mistake is trying to sew with the presser foot lifted. If this happens, check to make sure the thread is seated between the tension disks. Lift the presser foot and rethread the top thread path. Then, before you begin to sew, make sure the presser foot is lowered.

One of the nice things about newer electronic and computerized machines is that they won't let you sew with the presser foot up. You'll get a message to "lower the presser foot."

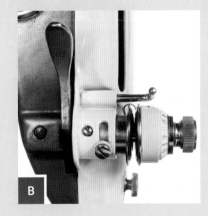

BOBBIN LOGIC

The purpose of a bobbin and how to install one correctly may seem very basic, but based on the number and kinds of questions I get from my students, many of whom consider themselves intermediate or advanced stitchers, it's worthwhile to explain what bobbins are and how they work.

Sewing machines create stitches by combining two separate threads. One thread is carried through the top of the fabric with the needle, while the other is fed through the bottom of the fabric from the bobbin. The bobbin is a little spool of thread that sits underneath the needle plate. As you sew, the needle is pushed through the fabric and catches the bobbin thread to make a two-sided stitch called a *lockstitch*.

STEP 1: Use the Right Bobbin

Use only bobbins that are made for, or are recommended for, your machine. I can't emphasize enough how important this is. If you use the right bobbin, you'll be much less likely to have problems sewing.

There are two common misconceptions about bobbins. One is that any bobbin will work in any machine. The other is that any metal bobbin will work in any machine that was originally shipped from the manufacturer with metal bobbins, or that any plastic bobbin can be used with any machine that was originally shipped with plastic bobbins.

Even if a bobbin seems to fit in your machine, if it wasn't specifically designed to work with it, it's likely to create problems. How do you know whether you're using the right bobbin? If you bought your machine new and use only the bobbins it came with, or if you use only the ones that came with your secondhand machine and they work well, then you're good to go.

But if you have a hodge-podge of bobbins you've inherited or purchased, do some research at your local sewing machine repair shop or search your machine online by its brand name and the model number (located either at the back or on the bottom, near the power cord) to confirm exactly what you need.

Standard bobbin case

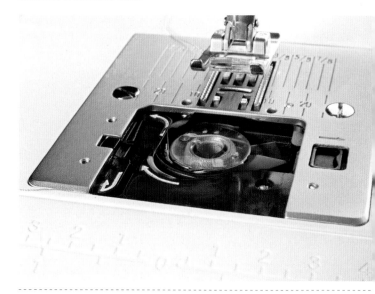

Drop-in bobbin case

STEP 2: Wind the Bobbin

Using the bobbin winder on the top of the machine, wind thread onto the bobbin following the instructions in the owner's manual.

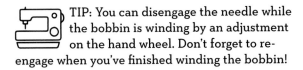 TIP: You can disengage the needle while the bobbin is winding by an adjustment on the hand wheel. Don't forget to re-engage when you've finished winding the bobbin!

Although all machines have the same elements for winding—a spool pin for holding the thread, guides for the thread as it winds its way to the bobbin winding spool, and a pretension device along the thread path to make sure the proper amount of thread is fed to the bobbin—the path of the thread will vary, so check the manual before you start. If you don't have an owner's manual, you can easily find a PDF online by searching for your machine's brand name and model number.

 TIP: Thread goes into the bobbin from the side and up through a hole in the top when winding, not from the top down!

STEP 3: Insert the Bobbin into the Bobbin Case

The bobbin case is a hardworking piece of precision machinery. Just as the spool pin and tension disks manage the steady flow of thread on the outside of the machine (see page 19), the bobbin case does the same inside the machine. The bobbin case has an area for the bobbin to spin and a tension-controlling mechanism to make sure the thread is flowing at an even pace.

In some machines, bobbin cases are separate and are usually loaded into the machine from the front; in others, they're integrated into the bobbin area, allowing you to drop the bobbin in and then guide the thread into place from above (hence the term "drop-in bobbin").

Either way, it's important to know that the bobbin case is a tension device. The tension comes from two separate areas: the tension spring on the bobbin case and the resistance caused by the redirection of thread winding off the bobbin in one direction and reversing into the notch under the tension spring in the bobbin case.

TIP: Once the bobbin is loaded into the bobbin case, and before you begin sewing, turn the hand wheel toward you until the needle is in its highest position. This will bring a loop of bobbin thread through the throat plate. Raise the presser foot and pull the thread up from the bobbin. The bobbin thread (and needle thread) should have a tail of thread at least 4" (10 cm) long.

The instructions and illustrations (see page 25) are general guidelines for inserting a bobbin into a case. Refer to the owner's manual for the instructions for your machine. Most newer machines have a graphic on the cover that shows how to insert the bobbin into its case.

Threading a Separate Bobbin Case

1. Hold the bobbin so the thread trails off in the opposite direction of the notch in the bobbin case (clockwise) (A).

2. Place the bobbin into the case, and then slip the thread into the notch in the case so it's going in the opposite direction (B and C).

3. Load the bobbin case into the bobbin area by pushing the bobbin case onto the bobbin pin until it clicks into place.

 TIP: After inserting the thread through the notch, listen for a little click as the thread sits down in the hole beneath the tension spring, and pull gently to make sure there's tension on the thread as it spools off the bobbin. If the thread doesn't pull out gently, then it might not be seated in the bobbin case correctly. With experience, you'll learn how much tension should be on the thread, and you'll be able to correct a tension or threading problem before you sew a stitch.

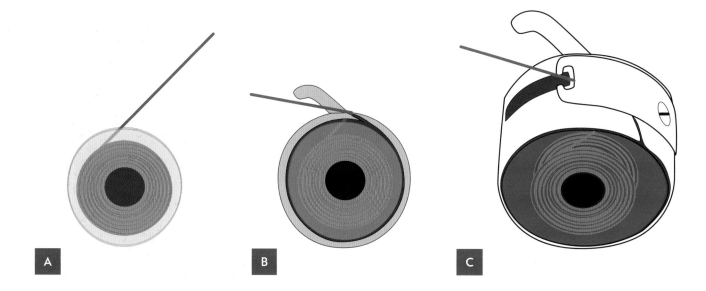

A

B

C

Threading a Drop-in Bobbin Case

1. Hold the bobbin so the thread trails off in the opposite direction of the notch in the bobbin case, or counter-clockwise (A).

2. Place the bobbin into the case (which appears to be an opening with a spool pin under the throat plate), and then slip the thread into the notch in the case so it's going in the opposite direction (B).

3. Wind the thread around the outside of the bobbin case, through the second notch and over the case (C).

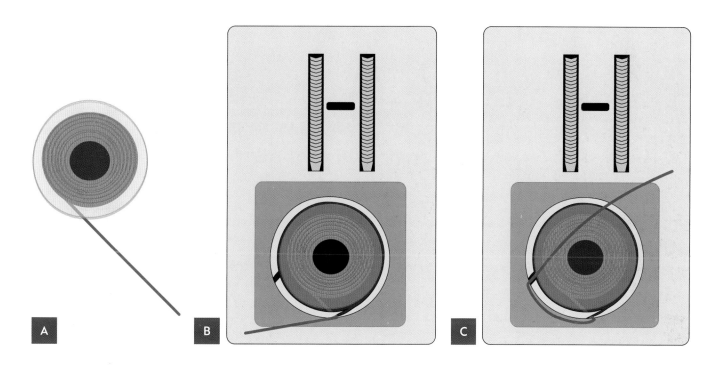

A

B

C

MUST-HAVE TOOLS

Here's a list of some of the basic sewing tools that belong in every sewing basket. You should gather them over time and keep them handy for all your sewing projects.

Awl—Use an awl to move fabrics through the machine without your fingers getting too close.

Basting thread—This is silk thread, but any brightly colored thread works.

Bobbins—Make sure bobbins are specific to your sewing machine.

Chalk—I recommend the wax-type tailor's chalk because it disappears with steam.

Cutting mat—Cutting mats are available in many sizes depending on your space and project needs.

Fabric marking pens—Fabric marking pens feature ink that is not permanent. The ink disappears over time, with the application of water or steam. They are wonderful tools for marking guidelines, cutting lines, and designs for decorative stitching or embroidery.

Hand sewing needles—Keep a selection handy for basting and finishing. I like sharps and betweens; they're small, sharp, and easy to use.

Marking pencil—Use this pencil to mark sewing details and keep your sewing oriented and on track.

Pinking shears—These cut a zigzag edge to finish raw edges inside a garment quickly, minimizing bulk. Old-school simplicity at its finest!

Pins—I prefer long, sharp quilting pins. They're easy to see and handle.

Rotary cutter—Not just for quilting, rotary cutters can be used to make bias tape and cut out patterns. You'll need a cutting mat to use a rotary cutter.

Rulers—Rulers are helpful for making patterns and marking hems.

Screwdriver—This comes with most machines and is used to attach presser feet and adjust tension.

Seam ripper—It's a good idea to have a few; they seem to fall in the wastebasket!

Seam sealant—Seam sealant is great for dabbing a tiny spot behind a freshly sewn button or on the cut end of a decorative trim so it doesn't fray.

Spring-handle shears—These are easy on your hands, as the spring does half the work.

Tailor's points 5" (12.5 cm)-long scissors—These are good for clipping corners and curves.

Tape measure—It's always good to have more than one tape measure on hand because they tend to get lost.

Thread snips—My favorite, Gingher thread snips, have a loop at the top of the cap so you can wear them around your neck on a ribbon or piece of twill tape. Great for keeping handy during fittings.

Tweezers—These are handy for grabbing thread after you've threaded the needle.

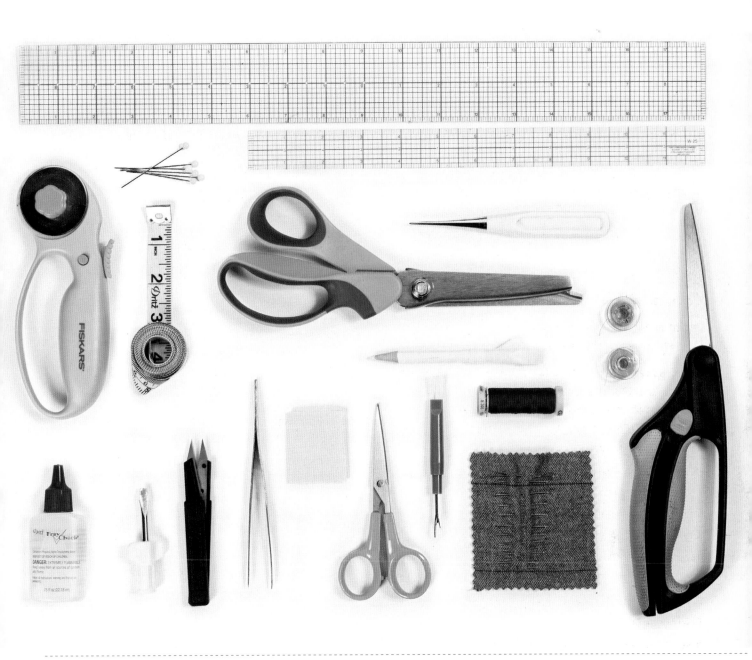

A selection of helpful tools.

NEEDLES

In addition to your sewing-basket tools, you should keep an assortment of different sizes and types of needles. They tend to break at the most inconvenient times!

Sewing machine needles are simple tools, yet they're calibrated to finely keep the stitches forming properly. This means that the slightest bend or barb in the needle can keep the machine from forming proper stitches.

Consider needles an expendable part of the sewing experience. They really should be changed with some regularity. People disagree on how often, so if you're having stitching issues and don't remember the last time you changed the needle, it's probably time for a new needle!

The weight and thickness of the materials affects the size and type of needle you should use. Keep in mind that heavier fabrics need larger needles. Needle sizes are 60/8, 65/9, 70/10, 75/11, 80/12, 90/14, 100/16, 110/18, and 120/19, with the large numbers suitable for heavier fabrics. Most sewing is done with 80/12 or 90/14 universal needles.

Different types of needles also help with different types of sewing. There are needles for denim and leather that are very strong and sharp. There are needles made especially for sewing knits and very densely woven technical fabrics, and there are needles perfect for sewing sheer fabrics. Here are a few popular needle choices.

1. Wing needles are used for decorative sewing to create holes in the stitchwork without cutting the threads. The wings on either side of the needle wedge between the fibers of the fabric and the stitch holds the holes open.

2. Twin needles have two (or three) needles on a single shank in a range of widths so you can stitch double or triple rows of parallel lines. They're great for reproducing the look of a coverstitch hem on a sewing machine.

3. Leather needles have a three-sided knifelike edge that is incredibly sharp. They're made to sew leather and vinyl with ease. The needle actually cuts into the leather, so don't backstitch. Do use a longer stitch length to keep the fabric from splitting.

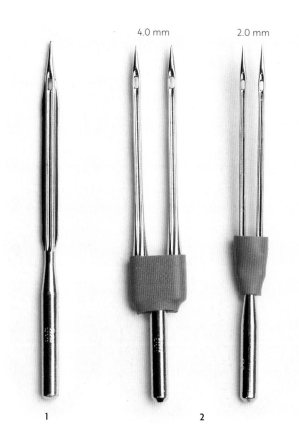

1

2

4. Denim needles are sharper and heavier than universals and have a slightly larger eye for stitching with heavier weight thread.

5. Stretch needles are designed to sew on stretch performance-type fabrics like Lycra and are used for sewing activewear and swimwear. They have a unique shape that keeps the machine from skipping stitches on super stretchy fabrics.

6. Universal needles are the go-to needle for most of your sewing. Your machine probably came with a universal size 80/12. Universals are suitable for most sewing with all-purpose thread and medium-weight fabrics.

7. Embroidery needles have a rounder and smoother eye, for use with lightweight embroidery threads and metallic threads. The smoother eye keeps the thread from shredding.

8. Microtex needles are extra sharp and thin for sewing on lightweight, densely woven fabrics such as microfibers.

Some other types of needles (not shown below):

Ballpoint needles are for sewing knits. If you are sewing a project with knit fabric, change to a ballpoint needle to keep from skipping stitches or poking holes in your fabric.

Quilting needles have a point designed to sew through multiple layers of quilting fabrics and batting with ease. It pierces through fabrics without punching the batting through to the outside.

Topstitch needles are designed to accommodate heavier, thicker threads. They have a bigger eye and groove for using heavier threads like buttonhole twist and 30-weight cotton.

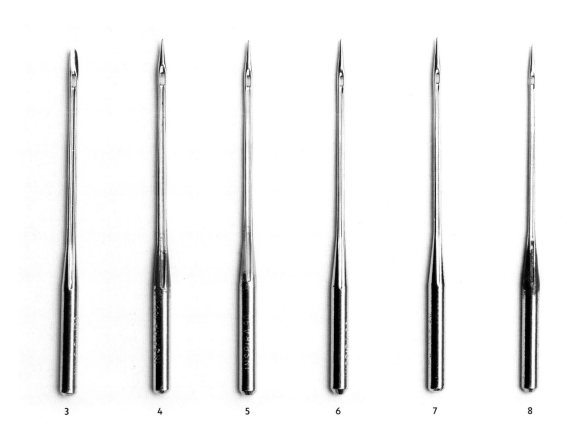

3 4 5 6 7 8

NEEDLE THREADERS

For years, I rolled my eyes at the idea of needle threaders, until I learned how well they actually work! I practiced a bit and found they saved me a lot of time—no more hunting for the needle hole when I'm threading my machine.

You can purchase manual threaders with clearly illustrated how-to instructions, but many of the newer machines have built-in needle threaders. You'll often discover that the extra bar and handle on the upper left side of the needle bar is actually a needle threader.

1. Raise the needle to the uppermost position.

2. Pull down the threader, using the handle on the left side. Align the hook so it is behind the needle.

3. Gently press the handle away from you so the hook pivots through the eye of the needle.

4. Hold the threader with your left hand and wrap the thread around the tiny hook just below the handle on the left. Keeping tension on the thread, pull it across to the needle hole (A).

5. Gently guide the thread upward along the tip of the needle until you feel the tiny hook grab the thread.

6. Holding the thread in your right hand, pull the threader handle toward you with your left hand. This pivots the hook and thread backward through the eye of the needle, leaving a loop of thread behind the needle.

7. Release the threader and thread and pull the thread loop from the back, threading the needle.

TIP: Built-in needle threaders are one of the most commonly repaired parts on modern machines. The part that is usually damaged is the delicate barb that hooks the thread, so be careful and don't move the needle while the barb is engaged, because it will bend or even break off.

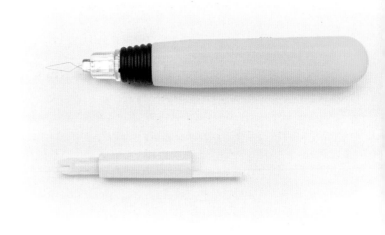

Needle threaders come in many shapes and sizes.

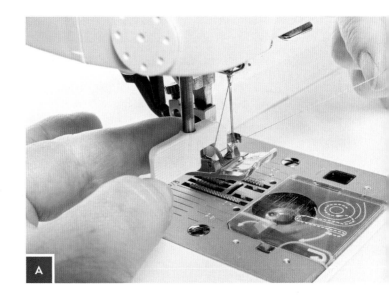

A

Threading Trick for Enclosed Feet

Sometimes, there's no slot for the thread in some enclosed presser feet, like a gathering foot, ruffler, chenille foot, or free motion foot. Here's how I manage the threads with a closed foot.

1. Hold the upper thread in your left hand and turn the hand wheel so the upper thread picks up the bobbin thread and pulls it through the top of the foot opening (A).

2. Draw up the bobbin thread and sweep it under the presser foot, catching the top thread. Tweezers might come in handy here (B)!

3. The top thread will follow; continue to sweep the threads under the presser foot (C).

4. Pull both threads under and to the left of the presser foot. Park the threads in the rear sewing position (D).

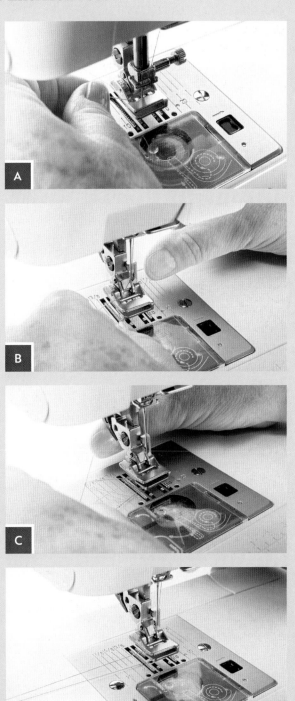

THREAD

A big factor in a smooth sewing experience is using the right thread for the job. You'll be surprised by how many different kinds of thread there are. I list them below from heaviest weight thread for heavy-duty sewing down to the finest and lightest weight threads.

1. Heavyweight/outdoor thread—Use heavyweight/outdoor thread for sewing canvas and other outdoor and water-repellent fabrics. These threads stand up to wet conditions better than all-purpose thread.

2. Upholstery, button, and carpet threads—These threads are heavy, but not as stiff as outdoor thread, and they are easier to work with because they're more like all-purpose thread, only thicker and stronger.

3. Topstitching thread—Topstitching thread is slightly thicker than all-purpose thread, and it is meant to be a little more substantive, so it is visible when used for topstitching. Gold topstitching thread, used on most jeans, is a great example; it's a bit thicker and stands out from the fabric.

4. Quilting thread—At about the same weight as all-purpose thread is 100 percent cotton quilting thread. Quilters tend to use this all-cotton thread to match the quilting cotton fabrics. Some people use all-purpose thread for piecing the quilt and all-cotton thread for the quilting. The logic is that quilters don't want the polyester thread to outlast or damage the fabric by its strength. This is an ongoing heirloom conservation debate!

5. All-purpose thread—For most sewing, it's good to have a selection of all-purpose thread. This thread is usually 100 percent polyester, or polyester wrapped in cotton. Polyester makes the thread thin but strong. This thread is suitable for garment, home décor, and most basic sewing tasks.

6. Silk thread—Silk thread is finer than all-purpose thread. I like to use silk thread for hand basting because it's very smooth and the silk fibers are very long. If you look very closely, cotton or cotton-wrapped all-purpose thread is a bit fuzzy; silk thread is less so. When used for basting, the silk thread slips through the fabric so you can baste quickly. Silk thread can also be dyed, so when I know I will be dyeing a garment, I'll sew with silk thread. The silk thread (and cotton thread, too) will take the dye and match the garment perfectly.

7. Embroidery thread—The thinnest, lightest weight thread is rayon embroidery thread. It's super smooth and shiny and makes pretty topstitching and decorative stitches that look more intentional. Embroidery thread also comes in several weight choices and an amazing array of colors.

Spools of every kind of blue thread and the stitches they make.

FABRIC WEIGHTS AND USES

Choosing fabric doesn't have to be difficult, but it is a very personal choice. Sometimes, it's the color that catches your eye, and other times it's the texture. Really, it's up to you! Just keep in mind the type of fiber (so you'll know how to launder it) and the weight of the fabric.

This chart of popular fibers, fabric types, and fabric weights makes the perfect source check when you are planning a project. There's no need to guess! This chart lays out fibers, fabrics, and weights so you'll know exactly what to buy!

NATURAL ↑ / **SYNTHETIC** ↓

Heavyweight ◄

Fiber Content				
Silk	Raw Silk	Dupioni	Taffeta	4-ply Crepe	Shantung
Wool/Cashmere/Mohair	Coating	Melton	Boiled wool	Bouclé	Tweed
Linen	Upholstery	Home Dec	Heavyweight		
Cotton	Canvas	Denim	Velveteen	Twill	Quilting
Bamboo	Denims (blended with cotton)			Fleece	Terry
Acetate	Drapery				Taffeta
Rayon	Ponte Knit		Jersey	Gabardine	
Spandex/Lycra	Jumbo Spandex	Ponte de Roma	Power Net		Novelty
Technical Fabrics	12–14 oz	10–12 oz		8–10 oz	
Polyester	Fleeces & Rainwear	Ponte Knit		Velvet	Satin
Nylon	Rainwear	Ponte Knit	Jersey	Jaquards blended with other fibers	
Acrylic	Sweater Knits			Knits, often blended	
Vinyl/Rubber	Marine Vinyl	Oilcloth	Tablecloth Vinyl	Heavyweight Neoprene	

OUTERWEAR	SUITINGS/ JACKETS	PANTS	CRAFT/ QUILTS	SKIRTS/ DRESSES	ACTIVEWEAR	HOME DÉCOR/ UTILITY	SHIRTS/ BLOUSES	HEIRLOOM	DANCE/ COSTUME	LINGERIE/ SHAPEWEAR	FORMALWEAR

→ **Lightweight**

Velvet	Crepe de chine	Charmeuse	China Silk (Habotai)	Tissue Faille		Organza	Chiffon
			Linings	Linings			
Suiting	Worsted	Gabardine	Suiting	Crepe		Tropical	Tissue Wool

Medium Weight			Lightweight		Handkerchief	
Broadcloth Poplin	Shirting	Muslin	Lawn	Voile	Organdy	Batiste
Jersey Knit		Single Knit	Organdy	Organza		

Lining			Organza	Drapery Sheers
Velvet	Challis	Bemberg Lining	Organza	Chiffon

Miliskin		Mesh Illusion	Stretch Lining
6–8 oz		4–6 oz	Capilene	2–4 oz

Gabardine	Crepe	Lining	Organza	Chiffon
Crepe	Tricot	Illusion	Laces	Organza	Net	Tulle

Knits, often blended		Hosiery	
Coated Nylon & Polyester	Lightweight Neoprene	Latex (can be natural)

INTERFACINGS, STABILIZERS, AND STAYS

Although invisible from the outside, interfacings, stabilizers, and stays make a big difference in the body, drape, and stability of a project. Think of it like a human body; the fabric we see on the outside is the skin, while the interfacings, stabilizers, and stays are like the skeleton and muscles, the inner support for the body/project.

Interfacings

Interfacings are lightweight materials that are permanently secured to the wrong side of the fabric. They can be woven, knit, or nonwoven constructions, and all constructions are either sewn or fused, with an iron, to the fabric. Typically, the heavier the fabric, the heavier the interfacing should be and vice versa. Although you might not need these products right away, tuck them away in your mental toolbox or keep an assortment handy. You'll find they will expand your creative potential (A)!

Stabilizers

Stabilizers, on the other hand, are often removed after stitching. Their purpose is to support the fabric so it doesn't shift or tear during stitching. They are often used for embroidery and decorative stitching (B). Stabilizers range in weight from whisper thin to heavyweight; choose the one that is heavy enough to support the fabric or light enough that it doesn't affect the texture or hand of lightweight fabrics. There are three types of stabilizers.

- **Tear-away stabilizer** is paperlike and usually lightweight. It is used under the stitching area, and any stabilizer visible once stitching is complete is easy to tear away.

- **Water-soluble stabilizer** dissolves in water and can be used to create lace on your sewing machine.

- **Melt-away stabilizer** is removed with heat from an iron after stitching is complete. It is a suitable stabilizer for terry cloth or other highly napped fabric because it keeps the embroidery design from getting buried in the loops of the fabric.

Stitches made on fabric with (left) and without fusible tricot interfacing.

Stays

Stays are strips of fabric, twill tape, or even elastic that are sewn into a garment during the construction process to help the garment maintain a desired shape. There are stay tape products that range from very thin mesh used to stabilize lightweight seams through to utilitarian cotton twill tapes of various sizes that are used to stabilize shoulder seams and necklines. Usually stays are used on areas of the garment that would stretch without the stay, such as the bias-cut edges of necklines, shoulder seams, and armholes (C).

TIP: You can use a line of stitching, called a staystitch, taken within the seam allowance to keep the edge of the garment from stretching before the garment is sewn. Staystitching keeps garments from losing their shape as the pieces are handled and sewn.

BALANCED STITCH FORMATION

A balanced stitch is the key to attractive and strong seams. The threads coming from the needle and from the bobbin require the correct amount of tension so they meet and loop in the middle, between the fabric layers. Most thread-tension adjustments are made for the needle threads; the bobbin tension is preset at the factory (A).

Loose Tension

The most common problem with stitch formation is looping on the underside. This is due to too much thread from the upper thread path; the needle thread tension is too loose (B and C). Refer to "Connection Between Tension Disks and Presser Foot" on page 21 to better understand how this happens.

The opposite problem, too much thread coming from underneath the stitching area and forming loops on the top of the fabric, is from lack of tension on the bobbin (D). This is usually caused by improper threading; try reinstalling the bobbin, making sure the thread is going in the right direction. See the illustration on page 25 for more information.

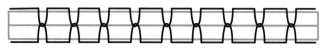

A

PROPER STITCH FORMATION

B

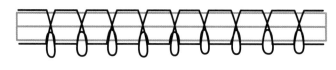

C

LOOSE TOP STITCH FORMATION

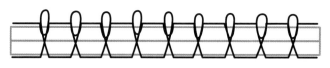

D

LOOSE BOTTOM STITCH FORMATION

Excess Tension

Too much tension on either the upper thread or the bobbin thread can cause stitches to pucker. The stitches should lie flat and smooth without distorting the fabric. In this case, the needle thread tension is too tight (E).

Reduce, or dial down, the needle tension. Do this by turning the dial on the upper tension disks, *in small increments*, usually by half a number at a time, so you don't end up making the tension too loose. Adjust the tension and then sew a test seam on a scrap of fabric. Keep doing this until you get a uniform stitch that doesn't pull the fabric too tight (F).

You'll rarely need to change the bobbin tension setting. If for some reason you do find that you have too much tension on the bobbin, first rethread the bobbin to make sure the thread isn't stuck on something (G). If this doesn't work and you need to tighten or loosen the bobbin tension, do that by adjusting the screw on the top of the bobbin case in very small increments. Remember the phrase: "righty tighty, lefty loosey!"

 TIP: Sometimes, instead of loosening the bobbin tension, you might try tightening the needle tension to compensate. It is always easier to adjust the needle tension than the bobbin tension.

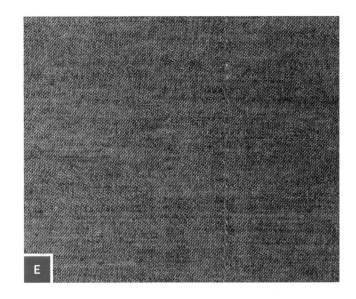

E

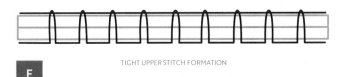

F

TIGHT UPPER STITCH FORMATION

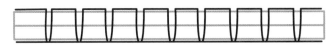

G

TIGHT BOTTOM STITCH FORMATION

TROUBLESHOOTING COMMON SEWING PROBLEMS

PROBLEM	REASON	TRY THIS	OR TRY THIS
Thread nests on bottom	Presser foot was raised so there was no tension on upper thread	After rethreading, make sure presser foot is down before sewing	If the presser foot is down and this still happens, then there could be a buildup of thread fibers in the tension disks. Try "flossing" fibers out with a piece of thread, or take the machine to a technician to address the problem.
Thread loops on bottom	No upper tension, thread not seated in tension disks properly	Remember to thread the machine with the presser foot lifted. Rethread upper thread using guide on page 18, make sure thread is seated in between the two tension disks	Adjust upper tension slightly until you have a balanced stitch
Thread loops on top	Not enough bobbin tension, thread not seated in bobbin case properly	Rethread bobbin using guide on page 20	Adjust, ever so slightly, the bobbin tension until stitch is balanced
No stitches form during sewing	Timing is off on machine	Rethread top and bottom threads; change needle	See a technician to address this problem
Uneven or skewed decorative stitches	Wrong presser foot for stitch	Refer to owner's manual for foot recommendations for particular stitches	
Fabric won't "feed" into machine	Feed teeth disengaged	Make sure feed teeth lever is in up position	
Machine is skipping stitches on knit fabric	Needle not right for the job	Replace with new ballpoint needle	
Machine is making holes in knit fabric as it stitches	Needle not right for the job	Replace with new ballpoint needle	
Thread is getting stuck or is too tight	Thread coiled around bobbin case and is stuck because bobbin is spinning in bobbin case; thread is coiled around spool pin on top of machine and getting stuck because spool spinning too fast	Bobbin is wrong size for machine; check to make sure it's the bobbin for machine's model number. Make sure there's a felt pad under the spool to keep it from spinning too fast; there should be one that came with the machine.	
Needle is breaking when using straight stitch foot	Foot and needle position are out of alignment	Make sure needle is in center position	Make sure presser foot holder and needle are securely attached to machine

STITCH SAMPLERS

Whenever I start a new project with a technique I've never done before, or when I am working on a project that will require me to toggle between techniques, I always make stitch samplers on the actual fabric that I am using to make the project. Once I have the stitches perfected on the samples, I make note of the stitch length and width and the tension setting or whether I used a special pressure foot. This is a great way to ensure smooth, even stitching for all of the construction processes.

You might want to keep your stitch samplers in a journal or on a bulletin board, so you can find them quickly and refer to them often (see below).

It's also a great, fun exercise to stitch out on fabric all the stitches your machine can perform so you have a visual reference of what's available on your machine. This is smart practice, and it lets you explore all your options without the pressure of a project.

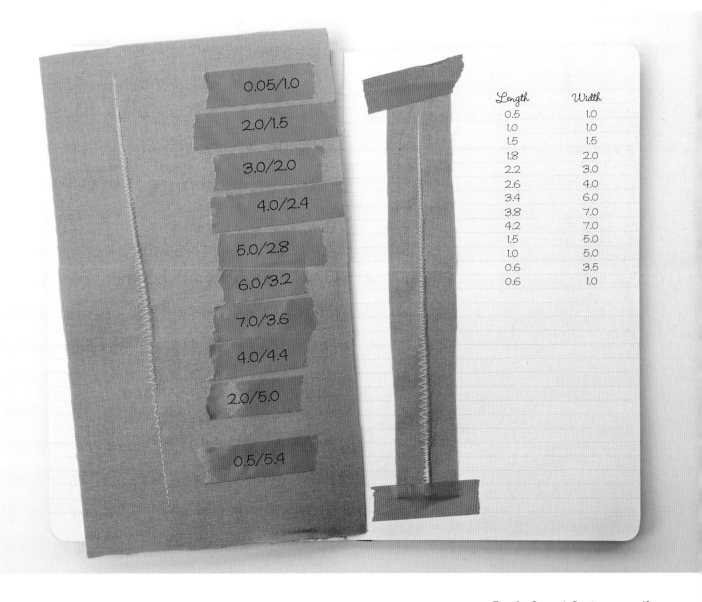

Length	Width
0.5	1.0
1.0	1.0
1.5	1.5
1.8	2.0
2.2	3.0
2.6	4.0
3.4	6.0
3.8	7.0
4.2	7.0
1.5	5.0
1.0	5.0
0.6	3.5
0.6	1.0

Labels on fabric sampler: 0.05/1.0, 2.0/1.5, 3.0/2.0, 4.0/2.4, 5.0/2.8, 6.0/3.2, 7.0/3.6, 4.0/4.4, 2.0/5.0, 0.5/5.4

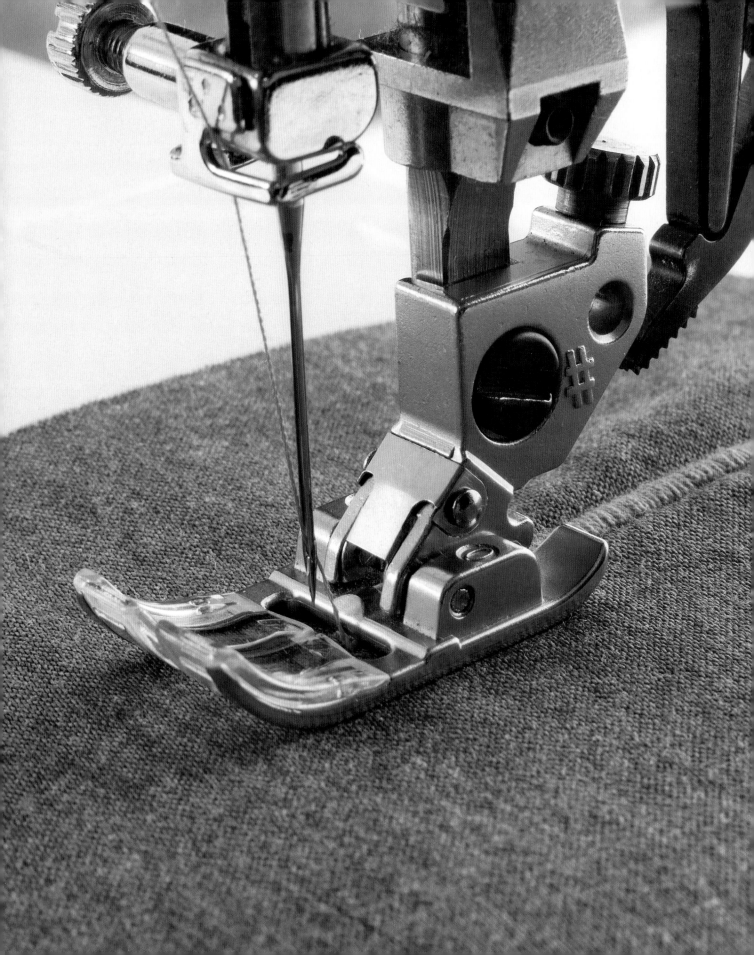

2

THE BASICS
STANDARD PRESSER FEET

Most sewing is done with the standard presser feet that come with your sewing machine. However, even though presser feet tend to look similar, they serve very different purposes and make a big difference in how a project turns out and how long it takes to complete.

In this chapter, you'll learn about the differences among the standard presser feet and how these feet can be used together to make a simple pencil pouch. The pencil pouch instructions, at the end of this chapter (see page 53), incorporate using the universal foot and the zipper foot, teach several sewing techniques, and help reinforce good sewing habits, all in the construction of one simple and useful project.

GENERAL OVERVIEW

Subtle differences in presser feet are the reason they produce better-looking stitches for specific tasks. One of the things that really throws people off when they begin sewing is how similar the various types of standard feet look. In the photograph at right, which shows three different styles of snap-on feet, it's easier to see the differences from the underside.

- The **universal/zigzag foot**, sometimes called the all-purpose foot (near right), has an opening that allows the needle to stitch both a straight line of stitches and a zigzag stitch, in which the needle swings from right to left.

- The **satin stitch foot** (center) has a larger cutout area for stitching wider, denser, and more dimensional stitches.

- The cutout section of the **decorative/embroidery foot** (far right) is the widest of the three shown here. As stitches become wider and denser, the amount of room under the presser foot needs to accommodate the buildup of thread.

So, while these feet look similar, the subtle differences in design are based on their intended functions. Theoretically, you can sew a straight or zigzag stitch using each of these feet, but when sewing satin or decorative stitches, it's best to use the foot designed for them, for the best results. You can also refer to your owner's manual for the manufacturer's recommendations on which foot to use with which stitch.

TIP: It is always a good idea, regardless of which presser foot you are using, to begin stitching a bit below the top edge, so the fabric doesn't get sucked into the machine. I often refer to this as "sinking the needle in the starting position."

When viewed from the underside, the differences among these three snap-on presser feet—(from left to right) universal/zigzag, satin, and embroidery—are easy to see.

Avoiding Common Mistakes: Stitch Length

One misconception that I run into frequently is that sewing with a really tiny stitch length makes a seam stronger. Actually, this just makes the stitching difficult and time consuming to remove (should that be necessary), and the stress of ripping out tight, tiny stitches might cause the fabric to tear. Use these settings as general guidelines for straight stitch lengths:

Fine tailoring and shirtmaking: 2.5 or lower

Seams: 2.5

Topstitching: 3

Basting: 4 and above

UNIVERSAL/ZIGZAG FOOT

The universal/zigzag foot is an all-purpose sewing foot that can be used with a wide range of needle and fabric types. In addition to straight stitch and zigzag sewing, the universal presser foot is well suited to many other stitch types and applications.

Variations in straight and zigzag stitches are made by lengthening or shortening the stitch length and width. Straight stitches have a width of 0 (zero), but can be many different lengths. Zigzag stitches vary in both width and length. This exercise lets you explore how to change from a straight to a zigzag stitch, and variations on both.

1. Attach the universal/zigzag foot to your machine.

2. Align the fabric edge with the ½" or ⅝" (1.3 or 1.6 cm, or whatever you prefer) seam measurement line on the stitch plate and lower the presser foot so it rests on the fabric. Hold both threads out of the way as you begin to sew. This prevents the threads from tangling on the underside of the fabric (A).

3. Stitch for a few inches (cm), then adjust the stitch length up or down to make longer or shorter stitches. (Seams are usually sewn at a stitch length of about 2.5; see "Avoiding Common Mistakes: Stitch Length" at left.)

4. Once you've established a good stitch length for your straight stitch, make a second line of stitches, only this time adjust the stitch width to create a zigzag stitch. Make a variety of adjustments to get the desired stitch width and length for your intended project (B).

5. Record your preferred stitch widths and lengths for future reference (see "Stitch Samplers," page 41). The sample shows straight (left) and zigzag stitches (right) made with the universal/zigzag foot (C).

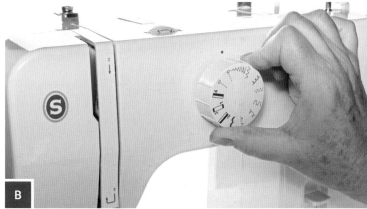

SNAP ON

LOW SHANK

HIGH SHANK

SLANT SHANK

BERNINA

STRAIGHT STITCH PLATE

Quilters like to use a straight stitch plate because the single hole in the plate keeps the needle from punching the batting down into the bobbin area when you're quilting. It is also great for sewing with delicate, slippery, or what I like to call "slimy" fabrics that wiggle around if you just look at them! Lightweight knit fabrics are also easier to sew with a straight stitch plate.

Just as with the straight stitch foot, the hole in this plate allows for more pressure on the fabric because there is only a single small hole for the needle. It's easy to switch between the standard stich plate and the straight stitch plate. You can set the machine only for straight stitching with this stitch plate; don't try to zigzag. *Remember to use the straight stitch foot with the straight stitch plate. Use the standard stitch plate for all other sewing.*

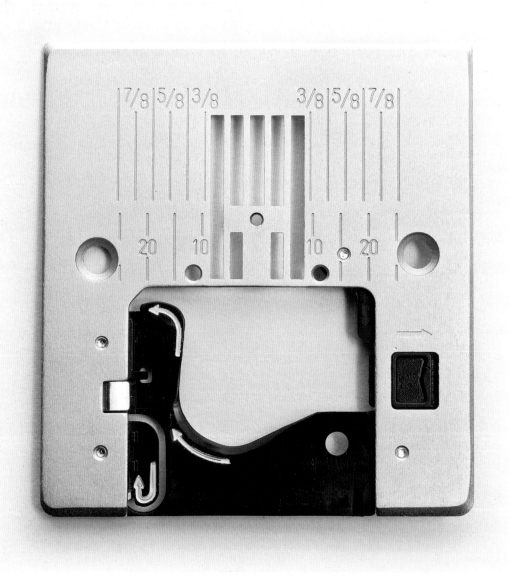

Straight stitch plate

1. Remove the presser foot (A).

2. Remove the bobbin case cover and the screws holding the stitch plate in the machine and set them aside. The screwdriver that came with the machine will work perfectly for this. Lift the standard stitch plate and set it aside.

3. If you notice lint in this area, it is a good time to wipe the area with a cotton swab.

4. Put the straight stitch plate on the machine, matching the feed teeth and screw hole openings (B).

5. Tighten the screws and make sure the stitch width is set at 0 for a straight stitch (C).

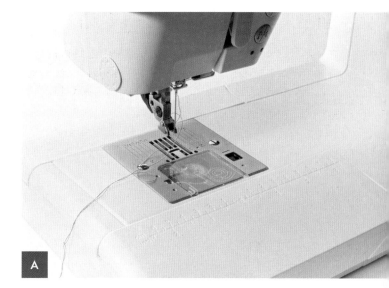

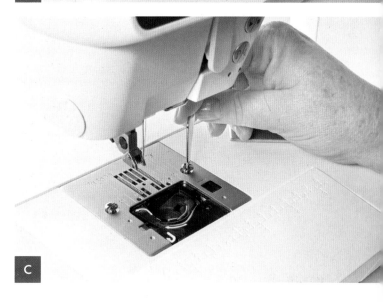

STRAIGHT STITCH FOOT

The straight stitch foot is designed to help with sewing fine, lightweight, or slippery sheer fabrics without puckering. It has a small hole for the needle and the rest of the foot is flat and smooth, so more of the presser foot is in contact with a larger section of the feed teeth, which helps move the fabric. This foot sews smooth and straight stitches because the small hole also prevents the fabric from getting pushed down into the needle plate opening during stitching. Make sure the machine is set for straight stitch; *do not try to zigzag stitch with this presser foot.*

1. If the machine has multiple needle positions, make sure it is set for the center position (A).

2. To avoid breaking a needle on the presser foot, slowly turn the hand wheel so you can see where the needle enters the presser foot hole. Once you've determined that the needle does indeed slip smoothly into the hole, you're ready to sew (B).

SNAP ON

LOW SHANK

HIGH SHANK

SLANT SHANK

BERNINA

SATIN STITCH FOOT

The satin stitch foot looks very similar to the universal/zigzag foot, but it has a wider opening on the underside to accommodate the buildup of satin stitches. Using the universal/zigzag foot for decorative stitching could cause a symmetrical stitch to appear asymmetrical and this might send you to the repair shop, thinking there's something wrong with the machine. The technician will put on the proper foot and your machine will work fine!

A

1. Install the satin stitch foot and set your machine for a zigzag stitch.

2. Shorten the stitch length to allow thread to build up but still travel.

3. Adjust the stitch width to the desired setting.

4. Lower the presser foot and test the stitch on scrap fabric in case you want to make adjustments to the length and/or width (A).

5. A sample with stitches made at two settings (B).

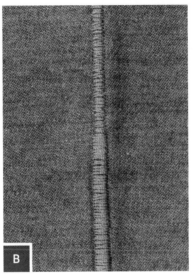

B

 **TIP: When you start a seam, you might want to set a narrow stitch width so you don't have to backstitch, and then, after two or three stitches, set it to the desired stitch width. This will eliminate bulk at the beginning and/or end of stitching.**

SNAP ON

LOW SHANK

HIGH SHANK

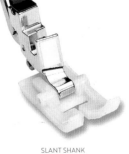

SLANT SHANK

BERNINA

STANDARD ZIPPER FOOT

The standard zipper foot can be used most certainly to install a zipper, but you can also use it any time you need to stitch close to, but not directly over, a zipper, seam, trim, or embroidery. The zipper foot has cutout notches on both sides so you can position it on either side of the zipper teeth (or trim, seam, etc.) and then adjust the needle position so you stitch exactly where you need to for the most control. Here's how to use the zipper foot to install a centered zipper. Refer to the zipper packaging for complete instructions.

1. Baste the seam closed with a universal or straight stitch zipper foot. Install the zipper foot and check that the needle fits smoothly within the cutout notches. You might want to take the time to make a practice stitch on scrap fabric to make sure the stitch length setting is correct.

2. Make any desired stitch adjustments.

3. Pin the right side of the zipper face down on the wrong side of the project with the zipper teeth centered over the seam. Baste the zipper in place.

4. From the right side of the fabric, lower the presser foot and sew with the edge of the presser foot along the zipper teeth a consistent distance from the basted seam (A).

5. When the stitching reaches the bottom of zipper, stop with the needle in the down position.

6. Raise the presser foot and pivot the fabric and sew across the bottom edge.

7. Stop with the needle in the down position and pivot the fabric again so that you can sew the second side of the zipper as in step 3.

8. Carefully remove the basting stitches from the seam so you can open and close the zipper (B).

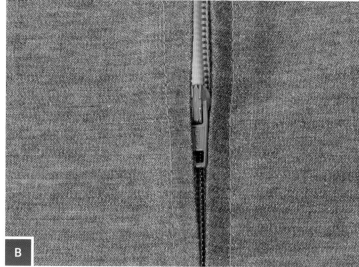

SNAP ON

LOW SHANK

HIGH SHANK

SLANT SHANK

BERNINA

OVERCASTING FOOT

The overcasting (or overlocking) foot is made specifically for finishing raw edges. It has a wire guide to help form the outer edges of overcasting stitches, thus duplicating the work of a serger or an overlock machine (A). The foot also keeps the thread tension from distorting the shape of the finished stitch, making a much neater edge than if you finished the cut edges with a standard zigzag foot.

1. Review the selection of overcasting stitches on your machine and select the one you would like to use. Install the overcasting foot.

2. Lower the presser foot and lower the needle into the fabric. Stitch slowly, keeping the guide on the presser foot running along the edge of the fabric (A).

3. The finished sample of overcasting stitches (B).

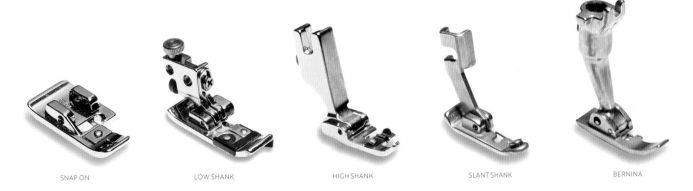

SNAP ON   LOW SHANK   HIGH SHANK   SLANT SHANK   BERNINA

PENCIL POUCH

This quick, easy-to-make pencil bag is perfect for keeping your favorite pencils and pens handy, and it's a great way to learn how to use a few of the feet discussed in this chapter. You will use a universal/zigzag foot to sew the bag and lining and a zipper foot to install the zipper. You'll use fusible interfacing to give the bag body and will learn how to make a boxed corner so the bag can sit up by itself.

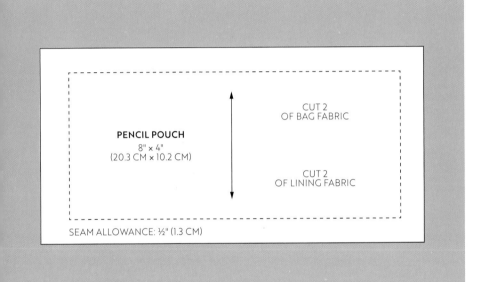

Finished size: 8" × 4" (20.3 × 10.2 cm)

Stitch type: Straight stitch

Length: 2.5

Width: 0

MATERIALS

¼ yd (.23 m) fabric for the bag

¼ yd (.23 m) lining fabric

¼ yd (.23 m) fusible interfacing

9" (23 cm)-long zipper

All-purpose thread

Iron and ironing board

Pins

Fabric marker or chalk pencil to mark stitching lines

ACCESSORIES

Universal/zigzag foot

Zipper foot

CUTTING THE FABRIC

See cutting diagram on left.

Use the diagram to cut 2 pieces from the outside fabric, the lining, and the interfacing.

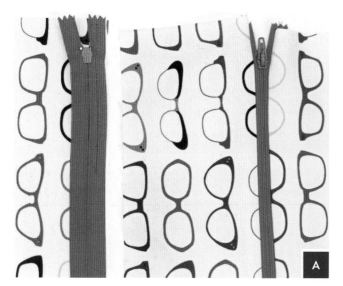

MAKING THE PENCIL POUCH

Unless otherwise noted, all seam allowances are ½" (1.3 cm).

1. Set aside the lining pieces. Fuse the interfacing pieces onto the wrong side of the outside fabric pieces, following the manufacturer's fusing instructions.

2. With right sides together, pin the zipper tape to one long edge of one of the bag pieces, edges aligned.

3. Install the zipper foot. Stitch the zipper in place with the edge of the zipper foot touching the left side of the zipper teeth (A).

4. Place a lining piece over the zipper, so all edges are aligned and the zipper tape is sandwiched between the bag and lining fabrics. Stitch directly over the previous stitching.

5. Press the fabric and the lining away from the zipper to enclose the stitching; the wrong sides of the fabric and lining will be together. Repeat with the remaining fabric, lining, and other side of the zipper (sometimes it is easier to do this with the zipper open) (B).

6. Close the zipper and fold the halves of the bag so that you can pin the fabric pieces with right sides together and also pin the lining pieces with right sides together.

7. Before stitching, partially open the zipper so you can reach in the bag to turn it right side out after stitching.

8. Sew all around the lining and bag, leaving an opening in lining, as shown (C).

9. Diagonally trim the corners of the bag and the lining (D).

10. Press the seams open.

11. To create the boxed corner, reach into each corner and align the bottom seam and the side seam together; pin. Stitch across each corner ½" (1.3 cm) from the point. Trim away the seam allowance (E).

12. Turn the bag right side out through the opening in the lining.

13. Hand or machine stitch the opening closed.

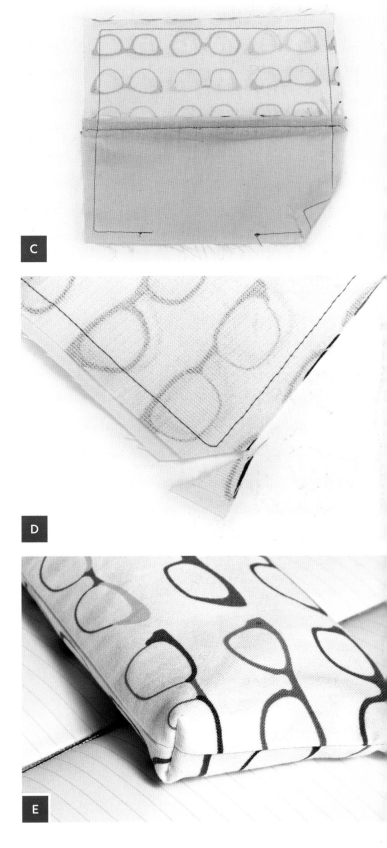

3

PRESSER FEET

FOR EFFICIENCY

Once you have learned the basics of sewing a seam, you can make so many things. You'll find repetitive tasks are easier and faster with the right tools, especially the right presser feet, and you'll be able to sew things by machine that in the past you would have sewn by hand.

It is important to know how to sew with old-school techniques, but for most projects, you can use time-saving tools like the button sewing foot, buttonhole foot, and elastic and gathering feet to do things that would take twice as long to do by hand. Even measuring buttonhole placement is easier and faster when you use a simple tool like the buttonhole gauge.

Twin needle (see page 67)

GENERAL OVERVIEW

Some of your time spent sewing will be dedicated to necessary, repetitive tasks, and that can take some of the fun out of it. I guess that's why I like gadgets and accessories so much, because once you get used to using them, you can't imagine going back to doing these time-consuming processes manually.

Button sewing and buttonhole feet are one of the best examples of this. They have been around so long that most people don't even learn how to make hand-worked buttonholes anymore. Those are saved for very special garments and can be gorgeous, but for everyday sewing, give me a great buttonhole foot and some good buttonhole choices. It makes all the difference, when you've worked hard on something, to have nice, crisp buttonholes and beautiful, uniform buttons.

Making ruffles and gathers can be tedious when you have to do a lot of them, but having a foot for that job makes you want to find places to put ruffles! When I think of all the petticoats and flounces I've gathered by hand, carefully so the thread doesn't break, or zigzagging over a cord and pulling. Sometimes, you still need to do it manually because it's in a very small space or only a small amount of fabric is involved, but if you're making costumes or kids' clothes, a gathering/shirring foot, an elastic foot, and a ruffler will be well worth the effort and expense.

The buttonhole gauge is something I keep finding new uses for! Every time I need to apply multiples of anything on a garment, I always grab that tool instead of measuring and dividing. It's so much easier to just count how many and mark top and bottom and all the increments in between. It's great for putting on military-style braid on uniforms or any other trim you come across.

If you've never used an invisible zipper foot to put in an invisible zipper, you are going to love how fast and easy they are. No wonder invisible zippers are so common in clothing now! When I hand off multiple dress projects to stitchers, the most frequent question is, "can I use invisible zippers?" They are really that much easier—and better looking, too.

Twin needles are the best thing for making and repairing casual clothing. So much activewear is now made using cover-stitch or coverlock machines that it's nice to have a twin needle to replicate that look without having to stitch everything twice and measure so carefully. I save up repairs and hems that require this sort of stitch and set up the machine with the twin needle. The hems come out looking much less homemade, and it's much quicker than a trip to the tailor's shop.

BUTTON SEWING FOOT

A button sewing foot is used to attach any flat button or closure that can be sewn to a project from the top. It's a big time saver if you have multiple buttons to sew on the same project and at the same time.

Be sure to set your machine for a zigzag stitch and to lower the feed dogs (unless your machine does it automatically; refer to your owner's manual). It's important that the stitch width is set so the needle goes back and forth through the holes in the button. You'll want to practice on scrap fabric. Increase the stitch width just a little at a time and lower the needle with the hand wheel. The stitch width is correct when the needle swings between and through the buttonholes.

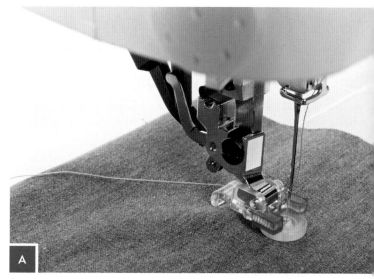

1. Mark the placement for all the buttons.

2. Place a button on the first marking. Lower the presser foot and use the hand wheel to lower the needle to double-check for clearance.

3. Set the stitch width to 0 and take a stitch to knot the thread. Change back to the stitch width needed to sew between the two holes of the button; begin stitching slowly so the thread crosses between and into the two horizontal holes until you have the desired look, usually five or six stitches (A).

4. If the button has four holes, raise the presser foot, clip the thread, and pivot the fabric and button to sew across the remaining holes (B).

SNAP ON

LOW SHANK

HIGH SHANK

SLANT SHANK

BERNINA

BUTTONHOLE FOOT

A buttonhole has two rows of parallel satin stitches connected at both ends with a bar tack. Most machines are able to make a buttonhole; refer to your owner's manual for buttonhole-making specifics. Making buttonholes has gotten much easier, and on some machines, it's just the push of a button—a far cry from buttonhole makers of yesteryear.

Mechanical machines are not automated, but they do allow you to make multistep buttonholes by turning a dial to reset the stitch width as you move between steps. Some mechanical machines have add-on buttonholers that are great if they are in good condition.

Electronic and computerized machines stitch buttonholes in one step. Your owner's manual will have precise instructions, but, generally, one-step automatic buttonholes are very easy to make:

1. Insert your button into the back of the automatic buttonhole foot. A sensor on the foot will then control the size of the buttonhole to fit the button (A).

2. Mark the buttonhole placement on the project with a disappearing ink fabric marker (see opposite).

3. Attach the buttonhole foot and lower the buttonhole sensor, if appropriate for your machine (B).

4. Lower the presser foot. Insert the needle into the fabric at the starting position for the buttonhole (C).

5. Begin sewing with either the foot pedal or a start/stop button. Stop when the machine finishes stitching and the needle returns to the up position.

6. A sample of completed button holes (D).

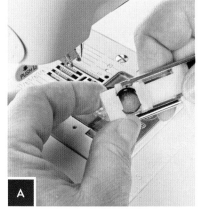
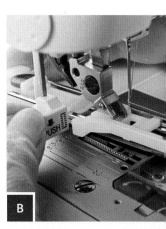

A

B

C

D

 TIP: Use a buttonhole cutter or a seam ripper to carefully open the buttonholes.

SNAP ON LOW SHANK HIGH SHANK SLANT SHANK BERNINA BERNINA

BUTTONHOLE GAUGE

In order to make sure your buttonholes are evenly spaced, use a buttonhole gauge to evenly mark placement with a fabric marking pen or pencil. You determine how many buttonholes or buttons you'd like to mark.

1. Determine the number of buttonholes you want on the project. Mark placement for the first and last buttonhole directly on the fabric with a fabric marking pen or pencil.

2. Count out that same number of prongs on the gauge as buttonholes.

3. Align the first prong with the first mark on your button area and the last prong with the marking for the last buttonhole on your button area.

4. Gently open the gauge so the remaining prongs spread out evenly between the two markings.

5. Mark the button placement in the notches at the end of each prong (A).

6. Make the buttonholes, starting each buttonhole at the marking (B).

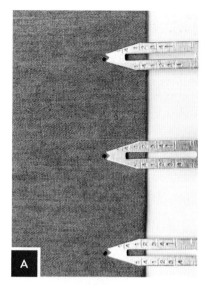

A

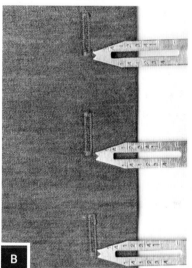

B

A buttonhole gauge is a metal accordion-type measuring device that allows you to mark placement for multiple buttonholes (or buttons) with equal distance between them.

TIP: If you don't have a buttonhole gauge, mark the desired number of buttonholes on a piece of ¼" (6 mm)-wide elastic, about 1" (2.5 cm) apart. Then stretch the elastic until the first and last marks on the elastic match the beginning and end of your button area. Transfer the markings from the elastic to the fabric.

ELASTIC FOOT

The elastic foot has a slot that holds the elastic in place while the fabric feeds through the sewing area.

1. Feed the elastic into the elastic guide on the foot and then toward the back to leave a few inches (cm) to hold onto when you attach the foot to the machine (A).

2. Set the machine for a stretch or zigzag stitch.

3. Stitch a few inches (cm) and make any adjustments needed so the stitch is balanced and the elastic feeds smoothly.

4. Finish stitching the seam, holding and guiding the elastic (B).

5. The gathers or shirring created are evenly distributed once the elastic relaxes (C).

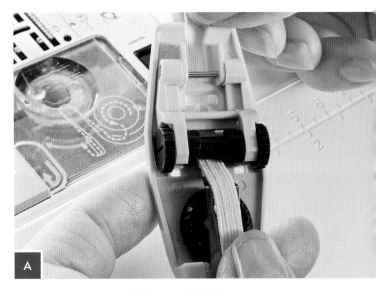

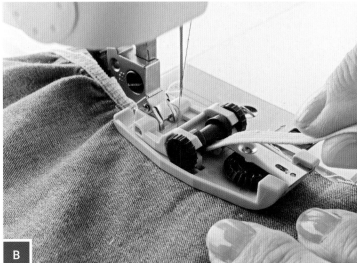

An elastic foot will help you attach elastic and gather a section of fabric all in one step. As long as you have an adaptor, this foot can be used with any type shank.

GATHERING/SHIRRING FOOT

The old-school way of gathering fabric is to run two parallel rows of basting stitches the length of the fabric being gathered and then pull the bobbin threads to make the gathers. A gathering foot makes it much easier: It uses the feed teeth of the machine to make the gathers. It's designed to slow down the movement of the fabric under the foot so that by lengthening the stitches, the teeth will move the fabric toward the needle quicker, creating a gathered stitch. You control the fullness of the gathers by adjusting the upper thread tension and the stitch length.

1. Set your machine for a straight stitch, with a 4.5 or 5 stitch length, and the upper tension set at 7. Refer to your owner's manual for the settings for your machine, particularly if the gathering amount doesn't suit your needs.

2. Lower the presser foot, and stack a bit of the fabric under the foot; hold your finger behind the foot to keep the fabric from flattening under the foot as you sew the first few stitches. When you see the machine start to make a gathered stitch you can move your finger (A).

3. Sew slowly, keeping the stitching line parallel to the edge of the fabric (B).

4. Be sure to stitch straight and far enough from the cut edge that the fabric doesn't get pulled into the machine (C).

5. Adjust the gathers farther, if neede, by pulling or loosening the bobbin thread.

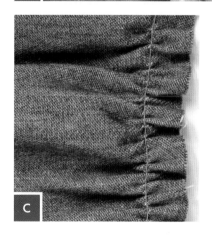

SNAP ON

LOW SHANK

HIGH SHANK

SLANT SHANK

BERNINA

RUFFLE FOOT

This foot creates evenly spaced pleats at measured intervals that are controlled by settings directly on the foot. The shank attaches to the presser bar. For machines with snap-on feet, you will need to remove the ankle and attach the ruffle foot with a screwdriver. The Bernina version has a low shank adaptor that attaches the ruffler to the machine.

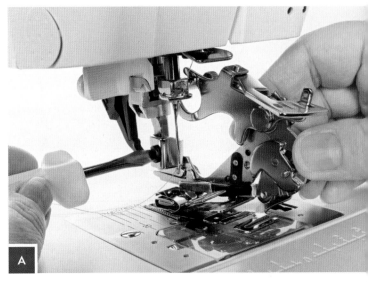

1. With the needle in the up position and the presser foot bar raised, attach the ruffle foot. To do this, guide the ruffle foot so the aligning hook arm straddles the needle bar on the right and the presser bar on the left; attach with the shank screw (A).

2. Make a practice sample to ensure the pleat depth and pleats-per-inch settings are okay. (See step 3 for inserting the fabric in the foot.) Fabric weight often requires some adjustment to the foot settings. Make small adjustments and restitch until you are sure the stitch settings work for the fabric. You might want to record these preferences in a journal, include the type of fabric, or even a swatch, in the notes.

   - Adjust the pleat depth by turning the screw on the foot, in front of the blade (B).

   - Adjust the number of pleats per inch with the gauge at the top of the foot (C).

LOW SHANK

HIGH SHANK

SLANT SHANK

BERNINA

3. Guide the edge of the fabric through the guides at the left edge of the foot, in and out. Then guide the fabric to the needle position by gently pushing the foot toward the sewing area.

4. Lower the ruffle foot and start stitching (D).

5. Raise the needle and the foot to the up position and remove the fabric, pulling it gently toward the back.

6. A sample of evenly spaced pleats (E).

C

D

Ruffle Math

It's not difficult to determine how much to gather your fabric: it's just math! Use the following ratios:

- **For minimal gathering:** 1 to 1.5 times the length of the fabric to which it will be gathered
- **For full gathering:** 1 to 3 times the length of the fabric to which it will be gathered

FOR EXAMPLE:
To add a gathered ruffle to a hem that is 40" (101.6 cm) in circumference:

- **For a full ruffle:** 40 × 1.5 = 60, so cut the ruffle 60" (152.4 cm) long.
- **For a very full ruffle:** 40 × 3 = 120, so cut the ruffle 120" (304.8 cm) long.

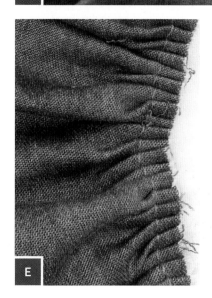

E

INVISIBLE ZIPPER FOOT

When they're installed, invisible zippers just disappear into the seam of the garment. When installing an invisible zipper, the presser foot does all the work of holding the zipper open and sewing the seam directly in the ditch beside the zipper teeth. It's amazing how easy this is.

1. Set your machine for a straight stitch and a 2.5 stitch length.

2. Open the zipper (press out any creases from the packaging).

3. Pin the top edge of the zipper seam with the right sides together. Open that seam and lay it facing up in front of you. Place the zipper right side down onto the seam opening. Pin zipper tape to the seam on each side. Unpin the seam and unzip the zipper.

4. Install the invisible zipper foot on the machine. Place the top of the zipper under the presser foot area and lower the presser foot. The V at the leading edge of the presser foot settles into the ditch next to the zipper teeth, as shown (A).

5. Lower the needle slowly using the hand wheel to ensure that the needle is centered close to the zipper teeth in the ditch next to the teeth.

6. Stitch along the edge of the zipper teeth a consistent distance from the edge of the fabric.

7. Stop stitching 1½" (3.8 cm) from the bottom of the zipper tape. Remove the fabric from under the machine.

8. Repeat steps 4–8 to stitch the remaining side of the zipper to the remaining seam edge.

9. Remove the invisible zipper foot and attach the standard zipper foot to sew the rest of the seam, with the right sides together and from the wrong side, starting where the previous stitching stopped.

10. Continue to sew the rest of the seam (B).

A

B

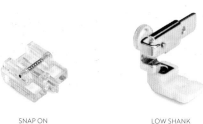

SNAP ON

LOW SHANK

HIGH SHANK

SLANT SHANK

BERNINA

TWIN NEEDLE

Twin needles are great for decorative stitching; they take the anxiety out of trying to keep stitched rows parallel. You can get twin needles with various widths between them, so if you're trying to match an existing stitch for an alteration, measure the width between the stitches to determine the needle size you'll need. You will also find triple needles for three rows of decorative stitching!

If you aren't using the same thread on both spools, make sure the threads you do use are comparable in weight. If you are using topstitching threads, which are heavier than all-purpose threads, set the stitch length at 3 for a slightly longer stitch.

1. Attach an extra spool pin (one probably came with your machine) and place a spool of thread on it and a spool of thread on the original spool pin (A).

2. Draw the threads off both spool pins equally and thread the machine with both threads at the same time, going through all the guides and the tension disks together (B).

3. When you reach the needles, separate the threads and let them hang down naturally to determine which one wants to be on the left or right needle. This helps keep the threads from tangling.

4. Hold the thread tails as you begin to sew; the bobbin thread will catch both upper threads as you stitch (C).

5. Sew normally with minimal backstitching, particularly if you are using topstitching thread (D).

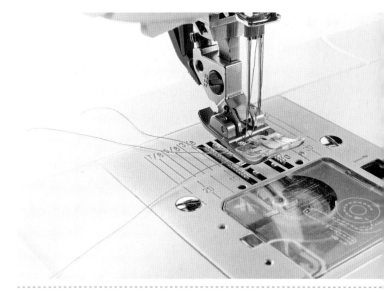

A twin needle features two needles on a single shaft, so you can sew two rows of parallel stitching at the same time.

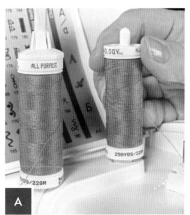

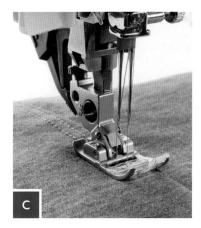

ZIPPERED CROSS-BODY BAG

This cross-body bag project incorporates many of the tools and techniques covered so far, plus a few extra sewing tips! To compete this project, you will use the standard/zigzag foot to sew the bag and lining itself, a zipper foot to sew the zippers, an edge stitching foot (chapter 4), or needle position for accurate topstitching. The long, parallel topstitching on the bag strap is made using an adjustable guide foot or a ¼" (6 mm) guide foot (chapter 4). Also, you will learn how to repurpose scraps from the zippers to attach the D rings, which give the bag a modern feel.

Finished size: 8" × 8" (20.3 × 20.3 cm)

Strap length: 26" (66 cm)

MATERIALS

⅓ yd (.3 m) of fabric for the bag

⅓ yd (.3 m) of lining fabric

⅓ yd (.3 m) fusible interfacing

1 yd (.9 m) of 1" (2.5 cm) grosgrain ribbon

3 zippers, 12" (5 cm) long

2 D rings

All-purpose thread

Pins

Iron and ironing board

Disappearing fabric marker or pencil

ACCESSORIES

Universal/zigzag foot

Zipper foot

Edge stitching foot (optional)

Adjustable guide foot or ¼" (6 mm) foot (chapter 4)

CUTTING THE FABRIC

See cutting diagram on left.

Use the diagrams to cut pieces from the outside of the bag fabric, the lining, pockets, and fusible interfacing.

CROSS-BODY BAG STRAP—H   27" × 2" (68.6 CM × 52 MM)

CROSS-BODY BAG FRONT—A 8" × 2.25" (20.3 CM × 5.7 CM)	CUT 1 OF BAG FABRIC CUT 1 OF INTERFACING
CROSS-BODY BAG BACK—D 8" × 2.5" (20.3 CM × 6.3 CM)	CUT 1 OF BAG FABRIC CUT 1 OF INTERFACING
CROSS-BODY BAG FRONT—B 8" × 2.5" (20.3 CM × 6.3 CM)	CUT 1 OF BAG FABRIC CUT 1 OF INTERFACING
CROSS-BODY BAG FRONT—C 8" × 4" (20.3 CM × 10 CM)	CUT 1 OF BAG FABRIC CUT 1 OF INTERFACING
CROSS-BODY BAG BACK—E 8" × 5.5" (20.3 CM × 14 CM)	CUT 1 OF BAG FABRIC CUT 1 OF INTERFACING
CROSS-BODY BAG LINING—F 8" × 8" (20.3 CM × 20.3 CM)	CUT 2 OF LINING FABRIC
CROSS-BODY BAG POCKETS—G 8" × 8" (20.3 CM × 20.3 CM)	CUT 3 OF POCKET FABRIC

This perfectly portioned bag has lots of pockets!

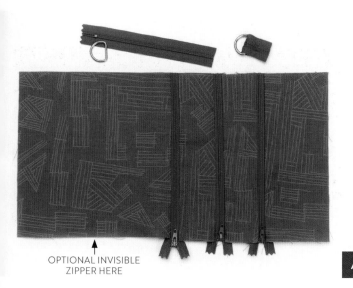

OPTIONAL INVISIBLE
ZIPPER HERE

A

MAKING THE BAG

Unless otherwise noted, all seam allowances are ¼" (6 mm).

1. Set aside the lining pieces. Fuse the interfacing pieces to the wrong side of bag pieces, following the manufacturer's recommendations.

Inserting Zippers

1. With a short zigzag stitch, stitch across the open ends at the top of each zipper to secure.

2. Apply the invisible zipper to back pieces D and E and treat this as one piece.

3. Install the standard zipper foot.

4. With right sides together, pin one zipper between pieces A and B and one zipper between pieces B and C. Stitch the zippers (see Making the Pencil Pouch, pages 54–55).

5. Pin the zipper between pieces A and D to form the top zipper and stitch (A).

Creating Pockets

1. Turn bag pieces to wrong side to expose zippers. Align a pocket piece to the bottom edge of each zipper and sew.

2. Press pocketing pieces away from zipper teeth and toward bottom of bag.

3. From the front side, topstitch ⅛" (3 mm) from edge of seam.

4. Fold up the pocket piece to meet the top edge of the zipper tape and stitch this edge. Turn to right side and topstitch from ⅛" (3 mm) from edge of seam (B).

Adding Loops

1. Baste edges of both pockets to sides of front of bag. Sew remaining lining pieces to top zipper as with the pocket

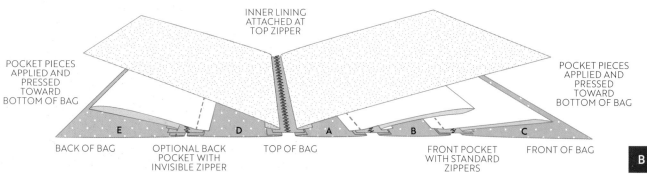

INNER LINING
ATTACHED AT
TOP ZIPPER

POCKET PIECES
APPLIED AND
PRESSED
TOWARD
BOTTOM OF BAG

POCKET PIECES
APPLIED AND
PRESSED
TOWARD
BOTTOM OF BAG

E   D   A   B   C

BACK OF BAG   OPTIONAL BACK POCKET WITH INVISIBLE ZIPPER   TOP OF BAG   FRONT POCKET WITH STANDARD ZIPPERS   FRONT OF BAG

B

pieces, enclosing the edges of the zipper opening and trim excess from zippers. Reserve two zipper scraps.

2. Loop zipper scraps around D rings with wrong side out to conceal zipper teeth (C). Sew to secure D rings and trim, leaving 1¼" (3.2 cm) from stitching line.

3. Fold lining for backside toward bag front to make sure not to catch it in stitches. Align D ring units along top of bag backside.

4. With a zipper foot to get close to D ring edge, sew around edges of tape to secure (D).

Adding Lining

1. Open top zipper and put right sides of bag together. Pin all around edges, making sure to pin into zipper seams at the top as in Pencil Pouch on page 54.

2. Pin lining together as well, as on page 55 leaving an opening at bottom of lining.

3. Stitch all around edges at ½" (1.3 cm) seam allowance, making sure to keep seam allowance straight at zippers and leaving bottom of lining open.

4. Trim corners as in Pencil Pouch (see page 55).

5. Press seam allowance all around, and stitch across 1" (2.5 cm) from outer edges to box them.

6. Trim points across corners and turn bag right side out through opening in lining.

7. Stitch across lining opening either by hand or by machine and arrange lining to inside of bag.

Creating the Strap

1. With right sides together, sew strap pieces together, making one long strip.

2. Press seam allowances to one side, edge stitch. Trim to ¼" (6 mm).

3. Wrapping entire ribbon with fabric and enclosing raw edge, press fabric around ribbon folding edge under and basting it down,

4. Using adjustable guide foot or 1¼" (3.2 cm) foot, stitch along whole edge of strap to finish and repeat to match along opposite side. Press.

5. Loop strap around bag hardware and sew with a narrow zigzag. Trim raw edges.

6. Attach a zipper pull to top zipper, if desired.

C

D

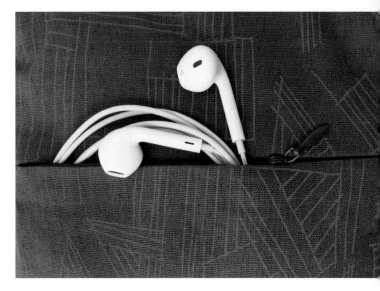

T-SHIRT WITH RUCHED COLLAR TRIM

One of the best ways to try out your new skills is to play around with something you already have and make it your own. For this project, you will use what you've learned so far to alter a T-shirt and add some charming details. You will use measuring tools, a gathering foot, and a button sewing foot. Note that the ruched trim is added only to the neckline of the T-shirt. Use a lightweight contrast cotton fabric, or fabric from a matching T-shirt, for the ruffle. Remember: This is *your* T-shirt, so if you want to add any kind of crazy trim, go right ahead!

Finished size: Varies by individual

Stitch type: Straight stitch for ruching step and bridging or feather stitch for joining and decoration

Length: Ruching: 5, joining and decoration: test for desired effect

Width: Ruching: 0, joining and decoration: test for desired effect

MATERIALS

New or gently worn knit T-shirt

½ yd (.46 m) woven cotton voile or batiste fabric

All-purpose thread, matching or contrast color

3 small buttons

Transparent 18" (45 cm) patternmaking ruler

Fabric marker or chalk pencil

Measuring tape

Pins

Fabric shears

ACCESSORIES

Universal/zigzag foot

Gathering or ruffle foot

Button foot

CUTTING THE T-SHIRT AND TRIM FABRIC

See cutting diagram on left.

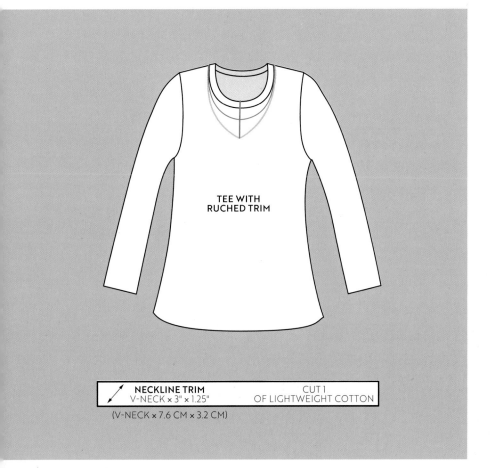

TEE WITH
RUCHED TRIM

NECKLINE TRIM
V-NECK × 3" × 1.25"   CUT 1
                    OF LIGHTWEIGHT COTTON
(V-NECK × 7.6 CM × 3.2 CM)

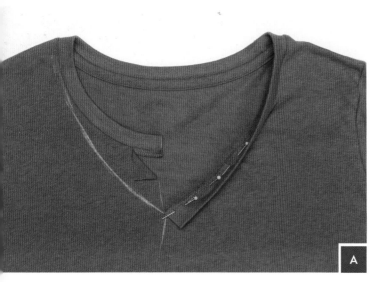

1. Lay out the T-shirt on a flat surface. Use the ruler to draw a vertical line from the exact center of the neckline to the approximate location of the new neckline. Use tailor's chalk, a chalk pencil, or a disappearing ink fabric marker so the design lines aren't permanent. With a measuring tape, measure your own body or one of your favorite shirts to determine how low you want to shape the new neckline.

2. Draw a new neckline, either rounded or V shaped. Make sure it is symmetrical. It helps to fold the shirt along the center marking and use chalk and pins to make sure the design lines follow the same shape.

3. Measure the new neckline so you can use the pattern provided to cut bias strips of fabric to make the neckline trim. Cut two bias strips, each being half the neckline measurement by 3" (7.6 cm) and 1¼" (3.1 cm) wide. You may have to cut multiple strips and stitch them together.

MAKING AND ATTACHING THE TRIM

Unless otherwise noted, all seam allowances are ¼" (6 mm).

1. Clip into the current neckline at the center front. Cut down along the center marking to the new neckline design line. Shape and pin the new neckline by folding and gently stretching the rib band over to the right side along the design line. The extra fabric will be trimmed away later. Overlap the cut ends of the rib band at the center V or seam the ends with right sides together (A).

2. Attach the gathering or ruffle foot to your machine. Gather each bias strip piece by stitching along one long edge. The edges of the ruffle pieces are unfinished, so they fray a bit over time (B).

3. Set your machine for a decorative stitch and thread it with matching or contrast thread.

4. Pin the ruched strips behind the neckband so that the ruffle barely peeks out from the neckline (the neckline edge will be trimmed later so more of the ruffle is visible).

5. Starting at one shoulder seam, stitch the trim to the T-shirt, pivoting at the V with the needle in the fabric. Continue stitching up the remaining side of the neckline (C).

6. Trim away the excess fabric from the old neckline that is folded inside the shirt. Trim off the edges of the rib band to better expose the trim and so it frays a bit. Use the button foot to attach the three small buttons, as shown (D).

7. If you wish, add a row of the same decorative stitches around the sleeve hem and the T-shirt hem to reinforce fraying, trimming, and the design (E).

 TIP: As the T-shirt is laundered, the ruched trim and other edges will continue to fray.

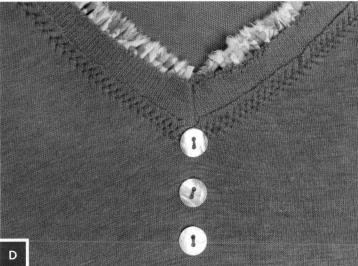

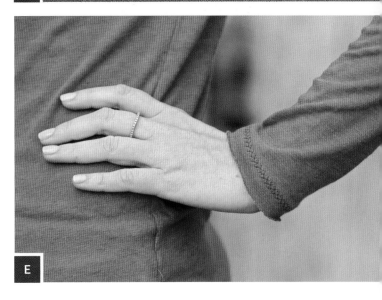

BOHO KNIT SKIRT

Skirts like this one are easy to wear and to make. The only drawback is sometimes, when you gather all that fabric into the waist, it makes your waistline too bulky. The method described attaches a gathered skirt to a smooth elastic waistband to streamline the look. To make this skirt, you will use the gathering foot and the overcasting foot and you will practice decorative stitching, using embroidery thread and a decorative stitch for the hem. You will also learn how to create a slim waistband and use a straight stitch plate for sewing with lightweight knit fabric.

Finished size: Your waist-to-ankle measurement

Stitch type: Straight stitch for gathering, overcasting stitch for overcasting step

Length: Gathering step: 5 or above and Overcasting step: test for desired effect

Width: Gathering step: 0 and Overcasting step: test for desired effect

MATERIALS

3 yd (2.7 m) lightweight knit fabric

1" (2.5 cm)-wide elastic, enough to wrap around your waist

All-purpose thread

Rayon embroidery thread for the hem

Measuring tape

Fabric shears

Pins

Ironing board

Iron

Fabric marker or chalk pencil

ACCESSORIES

Universal/zigzag foot

Straight stitch plate (optional)

Straight stitch foot

Gathering foot

Standard stitch plate

Overcasting foot

CUTTING THE SKIRT FABRIC

See cutting diagram on left.

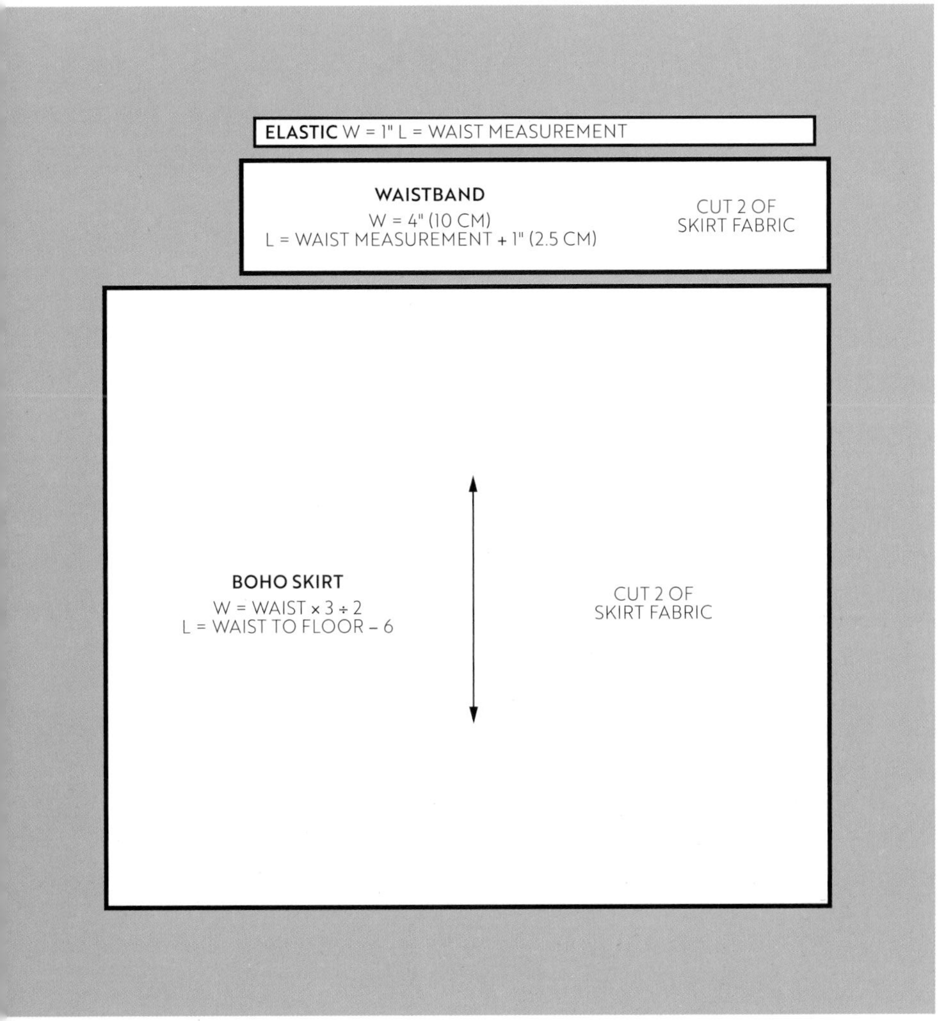

ELASTIC W = 1" L = WAIST MEASUREMENT

WAISTBAND
W = 4" (10 CM)
L = WAIST MEASUREMENT + 1" (2.5 CM)
CUT 2 OF SKIRT FABRIC

BOHO SKIRT
W = WAIST × 3 ÷ 2
L = WAIST TO FLOOR − 6
CUT 2 OF SKIRT FABRIC

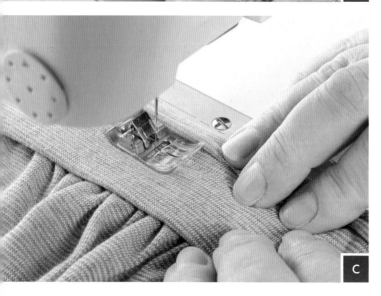

1. With a measuring tape, measure your waist and the distance from your waist to the floor. Make note of these measurements. Cut the fabric pieces as follows and according to the diagram:
   - Cut 2 skirt pieces, each (your waist measurement × 3 and then divided by 2) long × (your waist-to-floor measurement – 6" [15.2 cm]) wide
   - Cut 2 waistband pieces, each (your waist measurement + 1" [2.5 cm]) long × 4" (10.2 cm) wide
2. Cut a piece of elastic equal to your waist measurement.

MAKING THE SKIRT

Unless otherwise noted, all seam allowances are ½" (1.3 cm).

1. If you will be sewing with only straight stitches, switch to a straight stitch plate and straight stitch presser foot, especially if your fabric is lightweight.
2. With right sides pinned together and using all-purpose thread, sew the skirt side seams with a straight stitch. Press the seam allowances open.
3. Attach the gathering foot (and standard stitch plate) to the machine and gather the top edge of the skirt (A).

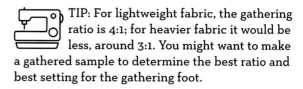 **TIP: For lightweight fabric, the gathering ratio is 4:1; for heavier fabric it would be less, around 3:1. You might want to make a gathered sample to determine the best ratio and best setting for the gathering foot.**

4. Overlap and sew the ends of the elastic together to form a loop; make sure the elastic isn't twisted.
5. Fold one narrow end of the waistband ½" (1.3 cm) to the wrong side. Fold the waistband fabric over the elastic, as shown. Overlap the folded end of the waistband fabric over the other end. Pin the fabric smoothly along the bottom edge. Stitch close to the edge of the elastic (B).
6. Use pins or a fabric marking pen to divide the waistband into quarters. The markings should represent the center front, center back, and side seams.
7. Use pins or a fabric marking pen to do the same for the top edge of the skirt; you will need to mark only the center front and center back.

8. With right sides together, pin the gathered edge of the skirt to the waistband, matching the markings at the center fronts, center backs, and side seams. Add pins between the markings to evenly distribute the skirt edge. Stitch the waistband to the skirt, stretching the elastic as you sew (C).

9. Gently stretch the waistband to pop any tight gathering threads (D).

10. Attach the overcasting foot. Stitch over the previous stitching. Trim along the edge of the overcast stitches; take care that you don't cut the stitches (E).

11. Press the bottom edge of the skirt 1" (2.5 cm) to the wrong side and pin.

12. Set your machine for an overlocking or decorative stitch and thread the machine with rayon embroidery thread; stitch as desired (F).

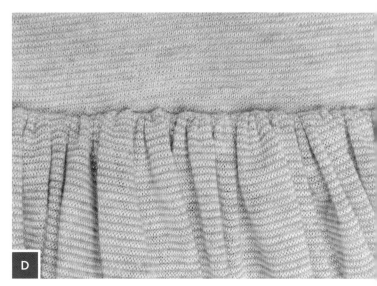

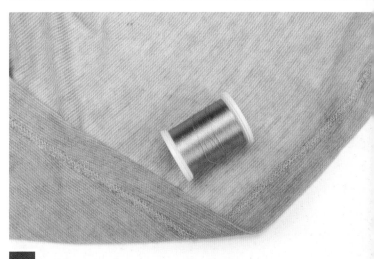

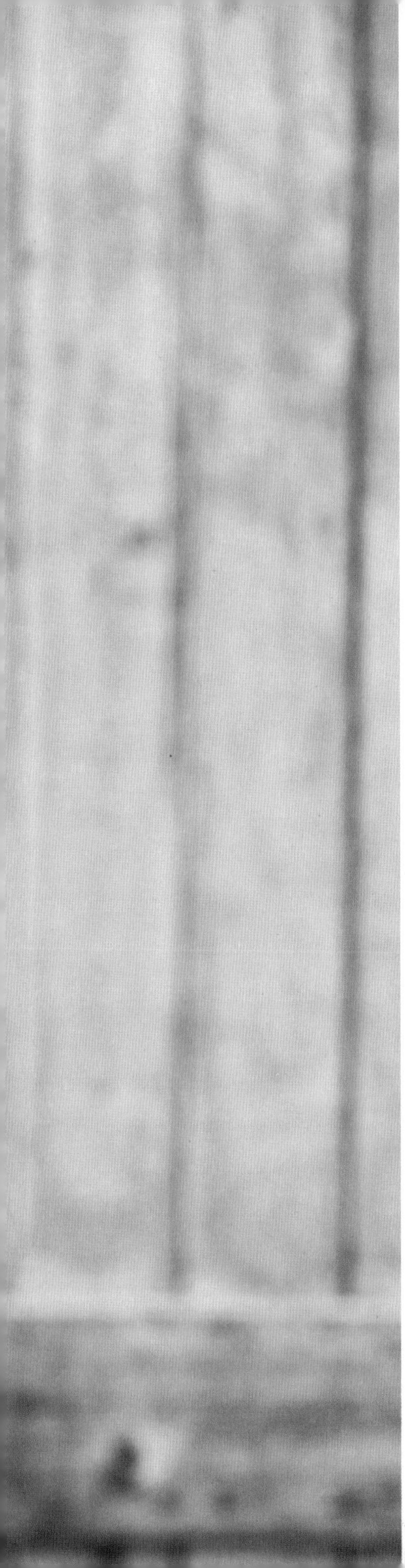

4
PRESSER FEET
FOR ACCURACY

If you walk into a factory of any kind, even bespoke tailoring shops, you'll find they can produce a predictably repeatable product because they have all the tooling necessary to do so. As I've worked with people from the apparel industry, costume shops, and couture workrooms, I've been fascinated by the "jigs" different people use—everything from oak tag strips used to get a perfect foldline on a hem, to machines set up for buttonholes and blind hemming, to sergers dedicated to a pearl edge calibrated to make a regular pair of tights into mid-century seamed stockings. The feet available for your machine are tools you can use to sew with exact precision.

GENERAL OVERVIEW

The human eye is pretty hard to fool. Sometimes, when a piece is supposed to be square and uniform and evenly distributed and it's not, it can be unsettling, especially if you are striving for the serenity of a beautifully executed, repetitive stitch detail. The presser feet and sewing tools described in this chapter will provide precision control over your sewing; once you know how they work, you will find all sorts of other uses for them.

Some people think of walking feet only for heavy or shifty fabric projects, but did you know that the waking foot is great for thin, slippery fabrics as well? Because they allow the fabric to feed evenly from the top and the bottom, walking feet feed whatever you're sewing much more accurately and make sewing anything tricky a lot easier and better looking.

The ¼" (6 mm) and adjustable guide feet are super useful for precision seaming and decorative stitching, and they take the wobble out of your stitching by using the edge of the fabric as your guide. They allow you to guide the fabric into the machine without having to wrestle your project from side to side, keeping it along the guides on the stitch plate.

Roller and nonstick feet are helpful in the same way as a walking foot in that they keep the material from grabbing the foot and causing wonky, uneven stitches.

All these feet can make your finished projects much tidier, especially in the finishes that can be seen from the outside, like with the blindhem and roll hem feet.

Edge-stitching and stitch-in-the-ditch feet are practical for the same reasons. They keep your stabilizing stitches used in facings and bindings looking either spot on the edge or hidden in the ditch.

I've included answers to the most frequently asked questions from my classes on these feet. Everyone always asks how to turn corners and curves with a roll hem foot, and I take you through that here. It just takes understanding and a little bit of practice.

WALKING FOOT

It is the feed teeth on the base of the sewing machine that pull the fabric through the area under the presser foot, creating forward motion. Sometimes, when you are sewing multiple layers of fabric—when you're quilting, for instance—the bottom and top layers feed unevenly. Or, if the fabric is very thin, there might not be enough traction with the feed teeth to pull the fabric through, resulting in a seam that's too tight.

A walking foot provides a feeding mechanism from the top of the fabric to work with the feed teeth underneath the fabric. Different manufacturers have different versions of the walking foot. Some are quite large, some just snap onto the presser foot bar, and some machines come with this sort of device built into the feeding system of the machine. Refer to your owner's manual for more information. Some Pfaff machines come with a built-in walking foot called IDT, or integrated dual feed, which goes both forward and backward in sync with the feed teeth (A).

1. Set your machine for the desired stitch.

2. Lower the presser foot and sew slowly, gently guiding the fabric with your hands. The presser foot will ensure the fabric feeds at the same speed (B).

3. The sample (C) shows a seam that's too tight (left) and one that was stitched with a walking foot.

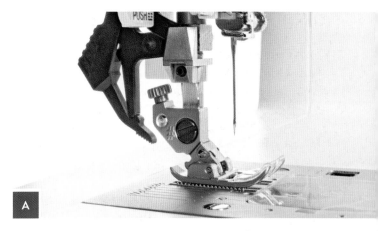

A

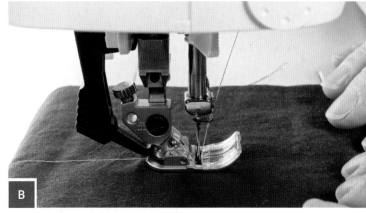

B

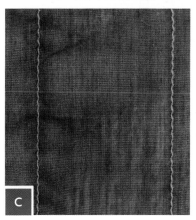

C

LOW SHANK
(REMOVE ANKLE OF SNAP SHANK MACHINE TO USE)

SLANT SHANK

BERNINA

(SEE BERNINA DEALER FOR BERNINA WALKING FOOT OR USE LOW SHANK WALKING FOOT WITH BERNINA ADAPTER)

¼-INCH GUIDE FOOT

The ¼" (6 mm) guide foot is a quilter's best friend. This foot is designed with markings and/or the size and shape to help you stitch consistent ¼" (6 mm) seam allowances. Some even have a metal edge to keep you from accidentally stitching seam allowances smaller than ¼" (6 mm). These feet come in metal or plastic versions. The clear plastic version is good because you can see through it to help turn precise corners. Apparel-production sewing typically uses a smaller seam allowance for precision, and this is the ideal foot for that need.

1. Set your machine for a straight stitch with a 2.5 stitch length. You might want to use the straight stitch plate.

2. Lower the presser foot so the needle is ¼" (6 mm) away from the cut edge and at the starting position (A).

3. Sew slowly, keeping the guide running along the edge of the fabric (B).

 TIP: Remember, when you are quilting, you don't need to backstitch at the beginning and end of the seams, as this can add bulk to your finished project.

A

B

SNAP ON

LOW SHANK

HIGH SHANK

SLANT SHANK

BERNINA

ADJUSTABLE GUIDE FOOT

An adjustable guide foot is exactly what the name implies: it has a sliding gauge that can be moved various distances from the edge of the foot to keep you from sewing beyond the seamline. This foot is nice because, just like with the ¼" (6 mm) guide foot, it prevents you from veering off the seamline, keeping stitches straight and uniform throughout the project. In my own experience, it also helps reduce eye fatigue caused by trying to keep your project aligned with the small measured grooves in the stitch plate. You can create your own low-tech version of this foot by placing a piece of removable tape on the stitch plate to act as a visual guide.

For measuring distances further from the needle than this foot, you can use a quilting bar that comes standard on even the most basic machines. Use it to sew regular rows of evenly spaced stitches, as with grid quilting projects, or whenever you want to stitch multiple parallel rows of visible and/or decorative stitching.

1. Set the machine for your preferred stitch type, stitch length, and stitch width.

2. Attach the adjustable guide foot. Measure the distance between the needle and the edge of the guide and adjust that distance by sliding the gauge as desired. Stitch a sample to make sure all the settings are correct.

3. Lower the presser foot and sew normally, making sure the fabric edge aligns with the edge of the foot as you sew (A).

4. A sample of multiple parallel rows of stitching (B).

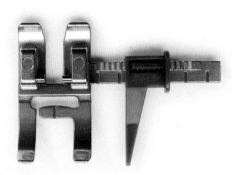

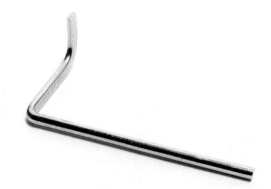

When used with the right shank adaptor, the adjustable guide foot (left) can be used with any type of machine. The quilting bar attachment (right) helps guide evenly spaced stitches.

ROLLER FOOT

A roller foot has rollers on the bottom that help fabrics move more easily through the machine. It is particularly well suited to working with heavyweight fabrics, including leather, vinyl, oilcloth, vinyl-coated cotton, neoprene, and thick polar fleece, as it helps prevent them from jamming, which can cause uneven stitches.

Depending on the fabric, you may also need a specialty needle, such as a denim needle or a leather needle. Leather needles are very sharp, with a honed knifelike edge that cuts through leather and other heavyweight fabrics. Be sure to keep your fingers out of the way if you sew with a leather needle!

When working with a roller foot, heavyweight fabric, or thicker thread, you will probably need to set your machine for a slightly longer stitch length to avoid stitches that are too small and tight. It's a good idea to make a stitch sampler to determine the best needle, type of thread, and stitch length for your fabric choice (see Stitch Samplers, page 41).

1. Attach the roller foot and your choice of needle.

2. Using your stitch sampler as a guide, set your machine for your preferred stitch, stitch length, and width. Sew as usual (A).

3. The roller foot will keep leather or vinyl from sticking to your foot and creating irregular stitches. A felled seam on oilcloth is easy to stitch using a roller foot (B).

A

B

SNAP ON

LOW SHANK

HIGH SHANK

SLANT SHANK

BERNINA

NONSTICK OR TEFLON FOOT

The nonstick or Teflon foot looks similar to a universal/zigzag foot, but it is made from a friction-resistant nonstick material similar to that used on cookware. This foot serves the same purpose as a roller foot in that it keeps fabrics like leather and vinyl from sticking and stretching out, and helps them glide through the machine as they're sewn to yield evenly spaced stitches of consistent lengths. Nonstick needle plates and nonstick sheets for covering the bed of the sewing machine are also available. These products are especially helpful for quilting and free motion embroidery.

It's a good idea to make a stitch sampler with the nonstick or Teflon foot to determine the best needle, type of thread, and stitch length for your fabric choice (see Stitch Samplers, page 41).

1. Attach the nonstick or Teflon foot and your choice of needle to the machine.

2. Using your stitch sampler as a guide, set your machine for your preferred stitch, stitch length, and stitch width. Sew as usual (A).

3. It is much easier to stitch a felled seam on oilcloth with a wide zigzag stitch using a nonstick or Teflon foot (B).

A

B

SNAP ON   LOW SHANK   HIGH SHANK   SLANT SHANK   BERNINA

BLIND HEM FOOT

The blind hem foot is designed to machine stitch a hem that is invisible from the right side. It has an adjustable guide that helps maintain the fabric position as you stitch. The blind stitch is a series of three or four straight stitches and one zigzag sewn from the inside, catching the edge of the outer fabric, making a hidden stitch. This foot is a real time-saver when hemming pants, skirts, and draperies.

It's a good idea to make a couple of samples on the actual fabric that you will be using to determine the best machine settings for the perfect stitch width and stitch quality. You will need to adjust the stitch width until the zigzag stitch just catches the fold. Record the stitch settings for future reference (see Stitch Samplers, page 41). There should not be any stitches visible from the right side.

1. The trick is to fold and press your fabric so you're forming all the stitches from the inside of the hem. Refer to the step-by-step folding illustrations (A, B, and C).

2. Set your machine for the blind stitch and adjust the stitch length and width, as determined by the test sample.

3. Attach the blind stitch foot.

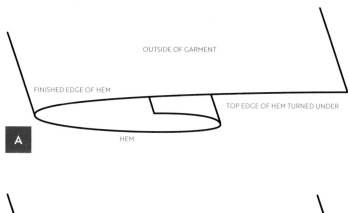

OUTSIDE OF GARMENT

FINISHED EDGE OF HEM

TOP EDGE OF HEM TURNED UNDER

HEM

A

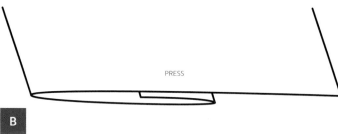

PRESS

B

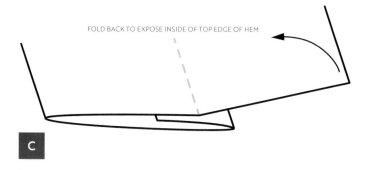

FOLD BACK TO EXPOSE INSIDE OF TOP EDGE OF HEM

C

SNAP ON

LOW SHANK

HIGH SHANK

SLANT SHANK

BERNINA

4. Position the fabric in the sewing machine to align the inner fold with the presser foot guide (D).

5. Lower the presser foot and stitch along the fabric edge so the straight stitches are on the inner edge of the hem and only the zigzag stitches catch the fold (E).

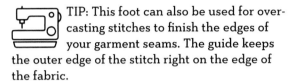 **TIP:** This foot can also be used for overcasting stitches to finish the edges of your garment seams. The guide keeps the outer edge of the stitch right on the edge of the fabric.

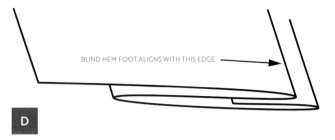

BLIND HEM FOOT ALIGNS WITH THIS EDGE →

D

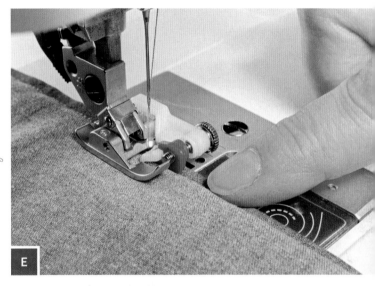

E

Presser Feet for Tidy Finishes

Some presser feet make it incredibly easy to stitch fine finishes with repeatable, predictable, and controllable results. Operations like hand sewing a hem with an invisible stitch and hand rolling a delicate hem can be done by machine quickly, easily, and, let's face it, without the need for manual dexterity! The blind hem foot and rolled hem foot (see page 90) are invaluable for stitching narrow hems on difficult fabrics.

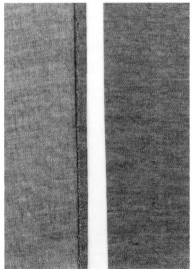

The only visible stitches are on the inside.

ROLLED HEM FOOT

The rolled hem foot curls the edge of your fabric back on itself and stitches close to the folded edge to make a great-looking finished edge. These feet are tricky to learn to use, but with practice they give you an elegant way to finish finer and slippery fabrics. They come in several different sizes, depending on the machine brand. The smaller foot is more appropriate for thinner, lighter weight fabrics and the larger ones are for thicker and heavier weight fabrics. It is a good idea to make a practice hem because every fabric type and weight behaves differently. You might want to record the stitch settings for future reference.

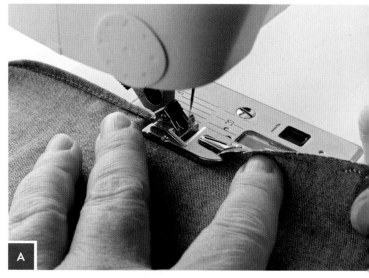

1. If you are starting on a corner, trim the corner at an angle so it is easier to guide the fabric smoothly into the foot.

2. Lift the presser foot and guide the fabric, as far as it will go, into the foot.

3. Gently lower the presser foot, making sure the fabric is making contact with the feed teeth.

4. Lift the edge of the fabric up with your right hand and use your left index finger to help preroll the fabric into the trough of the presser foot, in preparation for the roll (A).

5. Allow the machine to feed the fabric into the presser foot, rolling and stitching the hem. Stitch slowly enough to be able to control the fabric so the edge just rolls over and touches the left toe of the foot.

6. Stitch the hem (B).

SNAP ON

LOW SHANK

HIGH SHANK

SLANT SHANK

BERNINA

Turning Corners with a Rolled Edge Foot

1. Install the rolled edge foot and hem the first side; remove the fabric from the machine.

2. Trim a tiny bit diagonally off the corner and prepress a roll into the fabric before you begin stitching the second side (C).

3. Put the pressed corner *under* the presser foot, but not in the trough of the presser foot (D), and take a couple of stitches on your prepressed corner to get the rolled edge started. Holding the tails helps get the feed started (E).

4. With the needle down so you don't lose your place, lift the presser foot and feed the hem into the trough.

5. Lower the presser foot and proceed as you did for the first side, making sure to guide the fabric.

6. Repeat with each corner.

C

D

E

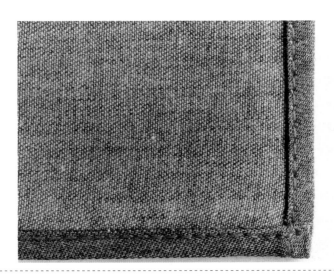

This technique produces perfectly square corners.

Hemming Curves with a Rolled Edge Foot

1. Begin the curved section the same as for a straight piece, by trimming the starting edge at a slight angle so it feeds easily into the foot.

2. Continue to stitch slowly, stopping periodically with the needle down. Lift the presser foot and pivot the fabric ever so slightly in the direction of the curve (F).

 TIP: The narrower the hem, the tighter the curve.

Tidy corners require practice, and any mistakes can be corrected.

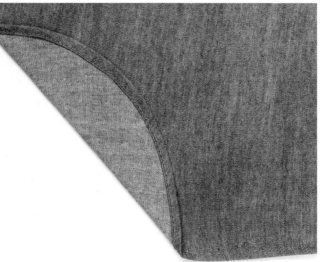

Practice on a piece of scrap fabric to get the feel of the presser foot before you hem your real project.

FELLING FOOT

The felling foot makes your projects look clean and professional. It's a great way to handle seams on a garment that won't be lined, such as a jacket or a shirt. This foot makes crisp, flat felled seams.

1. Pin or hold the two fabric pieces with the wrong sides together so the top fabric piece is about ¼" (6 mm) closer to the needle than the bottom fabric piece.

2. Stitch ½" (1.3 cm) from the edge of the bottom fabric piece (A).

3. Press the seam allowances open and then to the left.

4. Trim the beginning corner of the seam allowance at an angle so it fits into the foot more easily. Then press the first 1" (2.5 cm) of the wider seam allowance under to enclose the narrower seam allowance (B).

5. Gently lower the presser foot at the beginning of the seam and stitch a couple of stitches.

6. Stop and lift the presser foot and align the folded seam into the foot as shown. The foot will guide the rest of stitching to match the first part of the seam (C).

7. Allow the machine to feed the fabric in, rolling and stitching the seam down. Stitch slowly so you can control the fabric feed to make sure the edge is rolling over and forming the felled seam with a consistent seam width.

8. A stitch length of 3.0 makes a nice-looking felled seam (D).

A

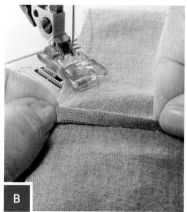

B

C

D

SNAP ON

LOW SHANK

HIGH SHANK

SLANT SHANK

BERNINA

EDGE STITCHING FOOT

The edge stitching foot has a guide that helps you sew close to the folded edge of the fabric. Edge stitching feet are also called stitch-in-the-ditch or joining feet. You can use any foot with a guide for the edge stitching process, including the blind hem foot or the adjustable guide foot.

Edge stitching is used a lot in garment sewing. It's the process of stitching multiple layers of fabric, usually to control the direction of seam allowances. On the inside of a well-made dress the neck facing and armhole facings will have edge stitching on the inside edge to prevent the facings from rolling to the outside.

1. Set your machine for a straight stitch with a 2.5 stitch length. Depending on the fabric, you might want to use a straight stitch plate for this stitch process (remember, lighter fabrics get sucked into the machine). See Straight Stitch Foot, page 48.

2. Lower the presser foot and sink the needle into the starting position, a bit below the top edge, so the fabric doesn't get sucked into the machine.

3. Stitch slowly, keeping the guide running along the edge of the fabric (A).

4. A clean line of stitching (B).

SNAP ON

LOW SHANK

HIGH SHANK

SLANT SHANK

BERNINA

STITCH-IN-THE-DITCH FOOT

The stitch-in-the-ditch foot allows you to guide your project through the stitching area, aligning a prior seam directly under the needle. For garment sewing, the stitch-in-the-ditch technique is most often used when making a waistband. It allows you to attach the inner layer of the waistband to the outside and keep that line of stitching hidden in the ditch of the seam.

In quilting, this foot is most often used in binding the edges of quilts or quilting exactly on a piecing line within the quilt design.

1. Prepare the seam by sewing a binding or waistband to the edge of the project and pressing the rest of the binding or waistband over the edge to enclose it. Use a few pins to make sure it doesn't shift.

2. Set your machine for a straight stitch with a 2.5 stitch length.

3. Sink the needle directly into the stitching (ditch) and lower the presser foot with the guide aligned with the seam (A).

4. Stitch slowly to better control the side-to-side movement of the fabric; you will have a completely hidden topstitch when you finish (B).

A

B

SNAP ON

LOW SHANK

HIGH SHANK

SLANT SHANK

BERNINA

CHENILLE FOOT

There are many great chenille projects, and using a chenille foot makes them fast and easy! With the chenille foot, you simply precut bias strips and the foot accommodates and stitches multiple layers of bias, all at the same time, to the base fabric. More importantly, you don't have to stitch in straight lines—you can stitch curves and shapes, as well.

However, if you want to stitch only straight lines, the low-tech (stack and cut) way to create chenille effects is probably faster. For this method, stack several layers of fabric and mark the bias grainline across the entire top layer in parallel lines. Straight stitch between all the marked lines, through all the layers. Then cut along the marked lines through all but the bottom layer. Machine laundering produces the frayed, chenille effect—the bias edge of the strips frays nicely!

1. Attach stabilizer to the wrong side of the base layer of fabric.

2. Draw your design directly onto the fabric using any kind of marker, because the design lines will be sewn over and won't show.

3. Cut enough bias strips to cover the design area, keeping in mind that you'll attach multiple strips each time you stitch. Make sure the width of the bias strips fit in the presser foot.

4. Load the chenille foot with three or four layers of bias strips before you attach the foot to the machine.

5. Set your machine for a straight stitch with a 2.5 stitch length. Attach the presser foot so the bias strips feed off the back by about 1¼" (3.1 cm) so you can grasp the strips as you start to sew (A).

A

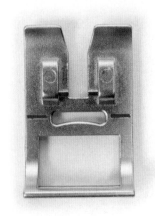

This presser foot is designed to guide and stitch layers of chenille strips to create a chenille effect.

6. Lower the presser foot and stitch slowly to manage the stack of bias strips, pausing with the needle down when you need to pivot at a curve or a corner to stay on the design lines (B).

7. Continue attaching bias strips until you've filled the design area (C).

8. Machine launder or manually fray the edges of the strips to create the desired effect (D).

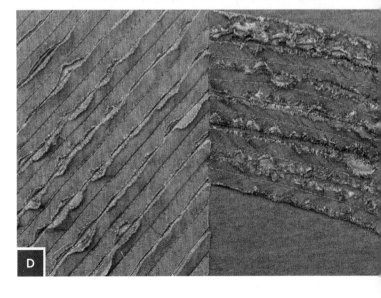

BINDING ATTACHMENT

A binding attachment is used to bind edges of garments or accessories by feeding perfectly folded bias strips through the sewing machine. The foot folds the binding and controls the fabric feed, so the machine can sew the binding to the both front and back at the same time. It's pretty handy, and it just takes a little practice!

1. Cut bias strips of fabric 1½" (3.8 cm) wide.

2. Set your machine for a straight stitch with a 2.5 to 3.0 stitch length.

3. Use a hand sewing needle to run a stitch through the tip of the bias strip. Then pull the needle through the foot to the back of the machine, pulling the bias strip into place slowly so the binding attachment creates a double-folded edge (A).

4. Once there are two folded edges extending from the back of the foot, place the fabric edge (to be bound) into the slot between the two folds of bias.

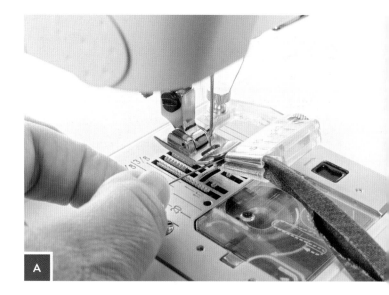

This bias marker is another one of those steampunk-looking devices often found among vintage sewing supplies.

SNAP ON

LOW SHANK

HIGH SHANK

BERNINA

5. Sink the needle into the beginning of the work area and slowly begin sewing, holding onto the bias extending out from behind the machine until the pieces are feeding smoothly (B).

6. Navigate curves by stopping with the needle down and pivoting to keep the fabric feeding smoothly into the foot (C).

7. To bind corners, sew all the way to the edge of the first side and then raise the presser foot. Tuck in and realign the bias on the second side. Start stitching again at the juncture of the edges at the corner. The miter can be sewn by hand afterward, if needed.

TIP: Make your own bias binding by using a bias marker, as shown here. It takes bias strips you cut yourself and folds them as you press with an iron. Pretty clever.

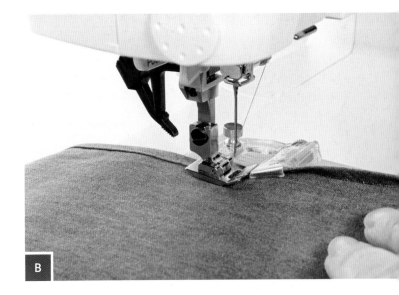

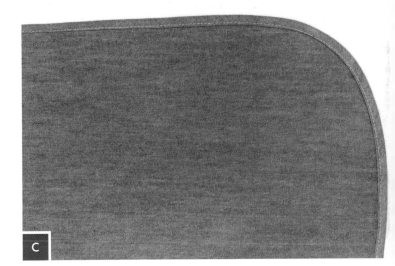

OILCLOTH GARDENING APRON

This simple project is a great way to try working with oilcloth or vinyl-coated cotton. Choose two contrasting oilcloth prints, plus a cotton fabric for the ties. I chose commercial bias tape for the binding, then found matching colored fabric for the ties.

Using a roller foot keeps the oilcloth from sticking and it rolls right over bulky seams. Although it isn't required, the ¼" (6 mm) guide foot makes it super easy to sew ¼" (6 mm) seams on the apron ties. To make it easier to bind the edges of the apron, I cut the basic shapes following the dimensions below, then I rounded the bottom corners by tracing around a cardboard spool approximately 3" (7.6 cm) in diameter.

Finished size: Fits waist circumference 30" to 42" (76.2 cm to 106.7 cm); Finished length is 11" (28 cm)

Stitch type: Straight stitch

Length: 3

Width: 0

MATERIALS

½ yd (.46 m) main oilcloth print

½ yd (.46 m) oilcloth in a contrasting color or print

¼ yd (.23 m) woven cotton

3 yd (2.7 m) precut and folded double-fold bias tape

All-purpose thread

Fabric marking pen

Fabric shears

Pins

Ironing board

Iron

ACCESSORIES

Universal/zigzag foot for sewing fabric ties

Roller foot when sewing steps with oilcloth

Optional: ¼" (6 mm) guide foot for sewing fabric ties

CUTTING THE FABRIC

See cutting diagram on left.

APRON TIES
24" x 4"
(61 CM x 10 CM)

CUT 2 OF COTTON

WAISTBAND
28" x 4"
(71 CM x 10 CM)

MARK CENTER ON BOTH SIDES

CUT 1 OF CONTRASTING OILCLOTH

POCKETS
26" x 8"
(66 CM x 20.3 CM)

MARK CENTER ON BOTH SIDES

MARK CENTER POCKET PLACEMENT 3" (7.6 CM) FROM CENTER

CUT 1 OF CONTRASTING OILCLOTH

PLEAT

PLEAT

APRON
24" x 9.5"
(61 CM x 24 CM)

MARK CENTER ON BOTH SIDES

CUT 1 OF MAIN OILCLOTH

MARK CENTER POCKET PLACEMENT 3" (7.6 CM) FROM CENTER

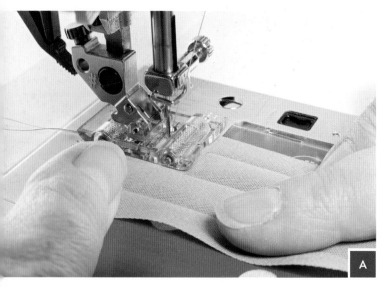

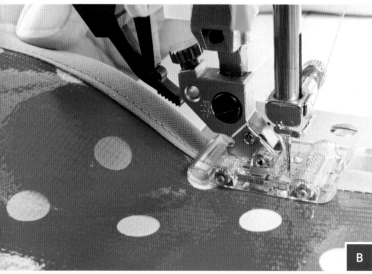

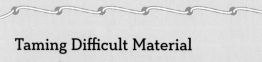

Taming Difficult Material

As an alternative to pinning, blue painter's tape or binder clips are great for securing vinyl pieces temporarily without damaging their surface.

MARKING THE CUT PIECES

1. Mark the center of both long sides of the apron, waist-band, and pocket, as indicated on the cutting diagram.

2. Mark the apron pocket at the bottom edge, 3" (7.6 cm) from each side of the center mark.

3. Make ¼" (6 mm) clips into the top edge of the apron ½" (1.3 cm) apart.

CREATING THE TIES

Unless otherwise noted, all seam allowances are ¼" (6 mm).

1. Fold each tie in half lengthwise with right sides together. If desired, taper the sewn end of each tie to a 45-degree angle. Using a ¼" (6 mm) seam allowance, sew along the length and one end. (Use the optional ¼" [6 mm] guide foot for this.)

2. Trim the corners of the seam allowance. Turn the ties right side out and press. Set the ties aside.

BINDING THE EDGES OF THE POCKET AND WAISTBAND

1. Cut and unfold a 28" (71 cm)-long piece of bias tape; align one edge of the bias tape with the upper edge of the pocket piece. Stitch along the uppermost foldline of the bias tape (A). Trim the bias tape even with the ends.

2. Fold the bias tape to cover the seam allowance, and fold it again to the wrong side of the pocket. If the bias tape doesn't fold down smoothly, trim the seam allowance slightly so it encloses the edge neatly.

3. Pin or clip the bias tape in place. Stitch along the bottom edge from the outside about ⅛" (3 mm) from the seam-line where the apron and bias tape meet (B). Set the pocket piece aside.

4. Repeat steps 1–3 to bind one long edge of the waistband.

CREATING THE POCKETS

1. Align the bottom edge of the pocket to the bottom edge of the apron, matching the center marks of both pieces.

2. Stitch the bottom edge of the pocket to the apron by sewing between the marks that are 3" (7.6 cm) from

each side of the center mark. Stitch vertical lines at each of these marks to the top edge of the pocket to create the center pocket, which is 6" (15.2 cm) wide. Backstitch across the binding to secure the stitching.

3. Align the outer edges of the pocket and the apron, making sure the bottom edges are also aligned. Pin or clip the edges together, keeping in mind that the bottom edge of the pocket is longer than the bottom edge of the apron. Fold a tuck, toward the center of the apron, at each mark on the bottom of the pocket as shown (C). Stitch at a ¼" (6 mm) seam allowance to create the outer pockets.

BINDING THE APRON AND POCKETS

1. Use the remaining bias tape to bind the edge of the entire apron and pockets, starting at the right side and going all around the outer edge. Clip into the seam allowance at the curves, as needed, to apply the bias tape smoothly.

FINISHING AND ATTACHING THE WAISTBAND

1. Fold the narrow ends of the waistband ½" (1.3 cm) to the wrong side. Then fold the waistband almost in half with wrong sides together so the bound edge extends about ¼" (6 mm) beyond the unbound edge. This makes it easier to ensure you catch the bottom layer of the waistband in the finishing seam.

2. Insert the open ends of the ties into the narrow ends of the waistband and create a little tuck in the center of each tie so they fit smoothly into the waistband (D). Insert the top edge of the apron between the folds of the waistband. Pin, clip, or tape all the layers together.

3. Topstitch all along the binding edge, enclosing the ties and the top edge of the apron in the waistband and being sure to catch the bottom edge of the waistband in the seam (E).

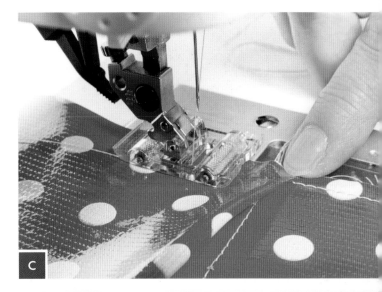

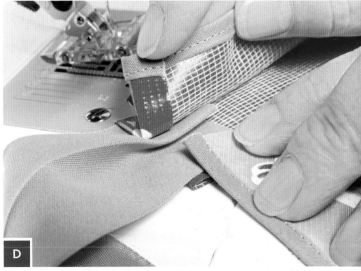

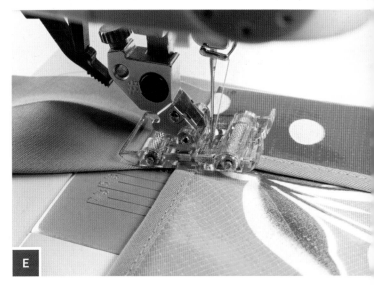

BABY BLANKET

One of the best things about being able to sew is making special gifts. A handmade gift is treasured and makes the art of sewing it even more rewarding. One popular baby gift is a faux chenille blanket. Sewing multiple layers of fabric together in channels along the bias grainline is one way to make them. Or you can try my method of making a more meandering organic pattern using a chenille foot.

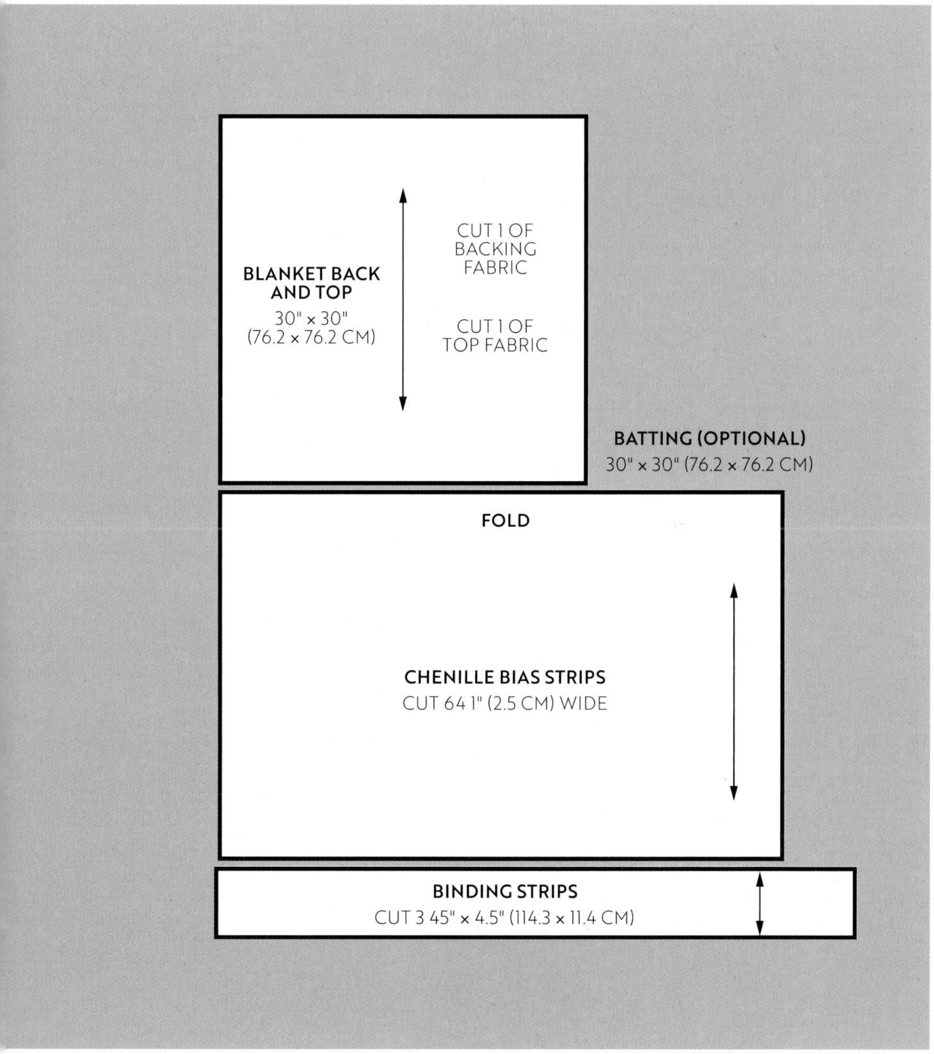

Finished size: 32" × 32" (81.3 × 81.3 cm)

Stitch type: Straight stitch

Length: 3

Width: 0

MATERIALS

1 yd (.9 m) top fabric

1 yd (.9 m) backing fabric

2 yd (1.8 m) fabric for chenille strips

¼ yd (.23 cm) binding fabric

Batting (optional)

All-purpose thread

Fabric shears

Ironing board

Iron

Basting spray

Pins

Blue water-soluble marker

Seam ripper

Hand sewing needle

ACCESSORIES

Universal/zigzag foot

Chenille foot

Edge stitching foot or stitch-in-the-ditch foot

CUTTING THE FABRIC

See cutting diagram on left.

BLANKET BACK AND TOP
30" × 30" (76.2 × 76.2 CM)

CUT 1 OF BACKING FABRIC

CUT 1 OF TOP FABRIC

BATTING (OPTIONAL)
30" × 30" (76.2 × 76.2 CM)

FOLD

CHENILLE BIAS STRIPS
CUT 64 1" (2.5 CM) WIDE

BINDING STRIPS
CUT 3 45" × 4.5" (114.3 × 11.4 CM)

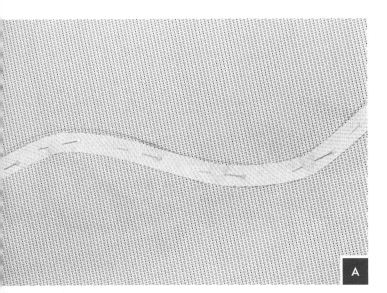

A

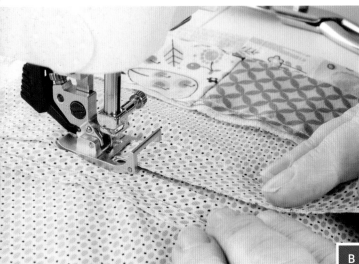

B

PREPARING THE BLANKET TOP WITH CHENILLE EFFECT

Unless otherwise noted, all seam allowances are ¼" (6 mm).

1. Press the blanket fabrics. Use basting spray to baste the blanket top and blanket bottom with wrong sides together. Add a layer of batting between the top and bottom fabric layers, if you prefer a loftier quilt.

2. Machine baste around the blanket top, ¼" (6 mm) from the cut edge.

3. In the center of the fabric, lay out and pin one chenille strip in a gentle curving pattern across the width of the fabric. Trace along the edge of the strip with a blue water-soluble marker to provide a guideline for attaching all the strips. This guide shows you how much the bias can curve without curling on itself (A).

4. Remove the pinned strip and insert a chenille strip in the chenille presser foot (see page 96). Baste in the center of the strip, following the guideline from step 3 (B).

5. Continue basting (longest strip length) strips to the fabric in the same meandering path, using the first strip as a guide. Be sure to baste all the strips as close together as possible.

6. After all the chenille strips are basted in place, covering the blanket top, attach the universal/zigzag foot. Adjust the needle position from right to left so you can straight stitch, with a stitch length of 2.5 between the basting and the raw edge of each strip. Be patient and stop and lift the presser foot, as needed, to keep the strips smooth.

7. Use a seam ripper to carefully remove the basting stitches from the middle of the strips.

8. With either a seam ripper or sharp scissors, cut through the center of each strip (where the basting was). Be careful to rip only the strips and not the blanket fabric.

9. Once the center of the strip starts to rip, it's easy to guide the seam ripper through the rest of the strip, effectively turning each strip into two strips.

SEWING AND ATTACHING THE BINDING

1. Trim all the outside edges so they are even.

2. Stitch all the binding pieces with right sides together and at 90-degree angles, to make one continuous binding strip.

3. Press one short and one long edge of the binding ¼" (6 mm) to the wrong side.

4. Beginning in the center of one side, align the unfinished binding edge with one top edge of the blanket. Start straight stitching with the machine set for a 2.5 stitch length, about 2" (5 cm) from the beginning edge of the binding. As you near the corner, stop stitching ¼" (6 mm) from the edge and backstitch.

5. Remove the blanket from under the presser foot. Fold the binding up and to the right, forming a 90-degree angle; finger press. Then fold the binding straight back down to the next edge, aligning the raw edges again. Begin sewing the next side of the blanket. Sew this side and repeat at each corner.

6. When you arrive back at the beginning, trim the binding, as needed, and tuck the unfinished edge just under the finished edge and stitch the rest of the binding in place.

7. Fold the binding to the back of the blanket and fold the corners diagonally to form miters (C).

8. Pin the folded edge of the binding in place (D).

9. Edge stitch the folded edge of the binding or use a hand needle to slip stitch the folded edge to the blanket. You can use the edge stitch foot or the stich-in-the-ditch foot.

10. Hand sew the corners closed.

FINISHING THE BLANKET

1. Rough up the raw edges of the chenille strips with a fingernail or a brush along the edges before washing.

2. Machine wash and tumble dry. Fabric softener helps fluff the fibers.

C

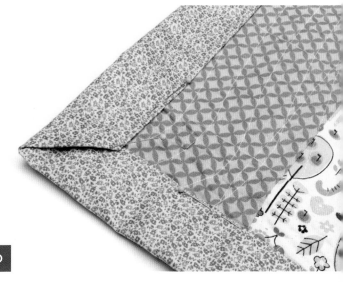

D

SIMPLE KIMONO

I love a great, simple jacket shape, and this kimono is one of my favorites. It's the most basic of all shapes, a T-shaped garment. The side seams flare out on this version as far as the fabric width will allow, to create an irregular drape and give the jacket a bit more swing. You could make this as a robe, as shown here, or with any sort of linen or heavier jacket-weight fabric for more of an outerwear version. The best feature is the strong vertical line down the front, making it so friendly for a curvy shape.

During the construction of this jacket, you will perfect stitching felled seams, using the edge stitching foot, and clipping into the seam allowances of curves for easier and smoother stitches. Refer to the cutting diagram on page 110 for help cutting out the pieces to make this functional and simple garment.

Finished size: chest up to 46" (116.8 cm), waist 56" (142.2 cm), hips 65" (165 cm), shoulder to hem 47" (119.4 cm)

Stitch type: Straight stitch

Length: 2.5–3

Width: 0

FINISHED KIMONO

Chest: 48" (12.9 cm)

Sleeve: (center back to wrist) 32" (81.3 cm), neck to hem (center back) 48" (121.9 cm)

MATERIALS

3½ yd (3.2 m) of 45" (114.3 cm)-wide fabric

All-purpose thread

Tape Measure

Transparent 18" (45 cm) patternmaking ruler

Yardstick

Curved dressmakers ruler (or round object) for shaping curves

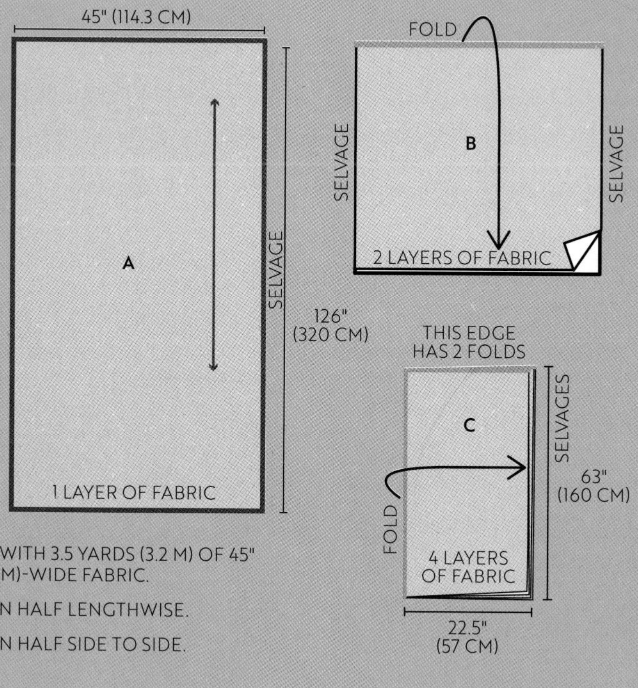

A. START WITH 3.5 YARDS (3.2 M) OF 45" (114.3 CM)-WIDE FABRIC.

B. FOLD IN HALF LENGTHWISE.

C. FOLD IN HALF SIDE TO SIDE.

FOLDING THE FABRIC

1. Start with 3½ yards (3.2 m) of 45" (114.3 cm)-wide fabric. Fold it in half lengthwise with the right sides together. Then, fold the fabric again in half from side to side. Refer to the folding illustrations at left.

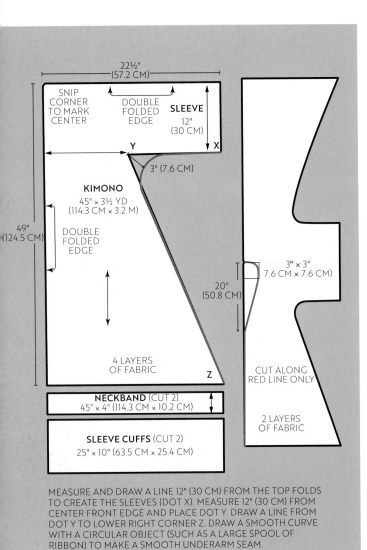

MEASURE AND DRAW A LINE 12" (30 CM) FROM THE TOP FOLDS
TO CREATE THE SLEEVES (DOT X). MEASURE 12" (30 CM) FROM
CENTER FRONT EDGE AND PLACE DOT Y. DRAW A LINE FROM
DOT Y TO LOWER RIGHT CORNER Z. DRAW A SMOOTH CURVE
WITH A CIRCULAR OBJECT (SUCH AS A LARGE SPOOL OF
RIBBON) TO MAKE A SMOOTH UNDERARM SEAM.

CUTTING THE FABRIC

1. Refer to the cutting illustration on the far left to mark the kimono cutting lines.

   - Measure and draw a line 12" (30 cm) down from the top folds to create sleeves (label X along open edge).

   - Measure 12" (30 cm) from the center from edge along the previously marked line and make a dot (label Y).

   - Measure 48" (122 cm) from upper left corner to bottom left corner and draw a line straight across for the hemline.

   - Draw a straight line from Y to the lower-right corner (label Z).

   - Use a round object to draw a curve for the underarm seam.

   - Make a small clip into the center upper-left corner to mark the center back of the neckline.

2. From remaining fabric, cut

   - Two neckband pieces, each 45" × 4" (114.3 × 10.2 cm)

   - Two sleeve cuffs, each 25" × 10" (63.5 × 25.4 cm)

3. Cut out the kimono, neckband, and sleeve cuffs along the marked cutting lines.

4. Unfold the fabric for the kimono once as shown in the illustration near left.

   - At the center back neckline snip, draw a 3" × 3" (7.6 × 7.6 cm) square with the fabric marking pen.

   - Measure from the center back neckline snip 20" (50.8 cm) along the center front fold.

   - Draw the neckline curve as shown. If you have a French curve, use it to draw the neckline.

   - Cut the center front open along the fold and then cut the draw neckline. *Do not* cut the center back fold.

MAKING THE KIMONO

Unless otherwise noted, all seam allowances are ½" (1.3 cm).

1. With the right sides together, sew the center back neck-band seam. Press the seam allowances open and set the neckband aside.

2. Set your machine for a straight stitch with 2.5 stitch length. Use the universal/zigzag plate and presser foot.

3. With the right sides together, pin the cuff to the sleeve opening so that the bottom seam allowance is ¼" (6 mm) wider than the top seam allowance (for a felled seam). Stich ½" (1.3 cm) from the outer edge. Repeat on the other side.

4. Install the felling presser foot. Press the wider seam allowance in half toward the wrong side for about the first 2" (52 mm) of the seam and start sewing with the felling foot. Stop stitching after an inch (2.5 cm) or so and place the felled edge into the foot. Continue to sew.

5. With the right sides together, pin the sleeve and under-arm seams so that the bottom seam allowance is ¼" (6 mm) wider than the top seam allowance (for a felled seam). Stitch ½" (1.3 cm) from the outer edge. Repeat on the other side.

6. At the underarm curve, trim away the shorter side of the seam allowance to ⅛" (3 mm) and the longer side to ⅜" (9 mm), blending into the original widths about 2" (52 mm) before the curve and 2" (52 mm) beyond the curve. (A) This will help the seam lay flat at the curve. Trim the sleeve cuff seam as well to reduce bulk at this juncture.

7. Stitch slowly at the curved underarm areas and sleeve cuff seams and pause occasionally to adjust the fabric beneath the presser foot to keep the seam straight.

8. Sew the remaining side seam and repeat on the other underarm seam (B).

9. Install the universal presser foot.

10. Press the edge ¼" (6 mm) to the inside and then press up the remaining 1" (2.5 cm) hem to the marking.

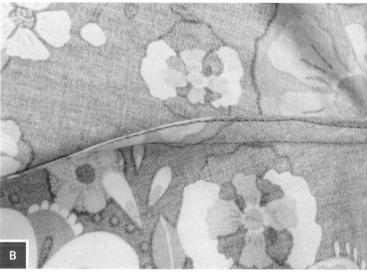

C

D

E

HEMMING THE KIMONO AND ATTACHING THE NECKBAND

1. Try on the kimono and pin up the hem to the desired length. Mark the hem on the inside of the kimono front. Trim away any excess length if needed, leaving 1¼" (3.1 cm) hem allowance. Press the edge ¼" (6 mm) to the inside and then press up the remaining 1" (2.5 cm) hem to the marking (C).

2. Miter the shaped hems at each side seam as follows (D). Press the side seam hem edges together to create a corner. Repeat with all sides, pinning to prepare to topstitch. Topstitching will keep the edges enclosed.

3. Press one long, raw edge of the neck band ½" (1.3 cm) to the wrong side.

4. With the right sides together, pin the unpressed edge of the neckband to the neck area matching the seam in the neckband to the center back marking on the neckline. Clip into the neckline seam curve to allow the seam to open freely for pinning and sewing. Make sure you don't clip past the seamline!

5. Continue pinning the neckband down the center front openings. Stitch the neckband to the kimono with a regular ½" (1.3 cm) seam allowance. The neckband will extend beyond the lower edge of the kimono. Press the seams toward the neckband.

6. Fold the neck band so the right sides are together at the hem edges and stitch across the neckband even with the hem edge. Trim the neckband ends at the front hem and turn the neckband right side out so the pressed edge of the neckband is on the right side of the kimono, covering the seam. Press.

7. Use an edge stitching foot to topstitch the open edge of the neckband in place, hiding the seam, around the entire center front and neck opening (E).

Basting for Smoother Topstitching

If you have trouble getting a nice, smooth topstitch while navigating pin removal, hand baste the area prior to topstitching. Just use a regular thread and hand sewing needle to make a long running stitch along the pinned area just off to one side of the stitching line, so you don't catch your basting stitches in your machine stitching. It takes a bit longer, but it's a great secret for smooth, beautiful topstitching.

5

PRESSER FEET
FOR CREATIVITY

Once you have learned the basics of what you and your sewing machine can do together and feel comfortable sewing "inside the lines," you'll be excited to learn about the presser feet featured in this chapter. These feet will take you on sewing adventures with decorative stitching and fabric manipulation. Now you can embellish those three-dimensional projects that you are making from two-dimensional fabric!

GENERAL OVERVIEW

Some of the presser feet, like the fringe foot, will guide and help you sculpt and add texture to your project. The open toe appliqué foot is cut out so you can see what you are stitching. And the free motion foot helps you better control the feed of the machine and use thread as a drawing and painting medium. Creative stitching is so much fun!

A lot of these feet for creativity give you ways to create new textures within the "canvas" of a sewing project, either with a wing needle making holes in the fabric in decorative, delicate, almost impossible-looking patterns, or making the fabric rise above its surface with the pintuck foot and twin needle.

Sometimes, you can break up a surface with design elements that bring disparate textures and colors together, like the couching and braiding foot that allows you to feed trim into the area under the needle as you sew making entirely new designs.

I love all of the embroidery feet, but my favorite of these is probably the free motion embroidery foot, because my grandmother showed me how she made monograms with it when I was a little girl. She had a machine in a cabinet that I'm certain she probably paid for on lay-away and made beautiful monogrammed pillowcases as gifts. She had a way of making everything beautiful.

It always amazed me that you could do that with a sewing machine, by dropping the feed dogs and going out of bounds. I think that's why people love using these for free motion quilting, too. It's really fun!

EMBROIDERY FOOT

The embroidery foot looks like the standard zigzag and satin stitch foot from earlier, but the underside has a wider cutout for the build-up of stitches to pass through. This foot usually comes standard with most machines that feature decorative stitch capabilities. It's important to use this foot so the stitch is balanced from left to right. Using a standard foot for decorative stitching could distort the stitches, making you think there is a problem with your machine.

1. Choose a decorative stitch from the stitch selection and reference manual; your machine should then indicate the best stitch length and width settings. You might want to use a fabric marking pen to draw a stitching guideline.

2. Consider applying stabilizer to the wrong side of lightweight fabrics to keep the stitches from puckering (A).

3. Stitch the line of decorative stitches, letting the machine feed the fabric. There is no need to pull or manipulate the fabric—just gently guide it, as needed, to stay on the stitching line (B).

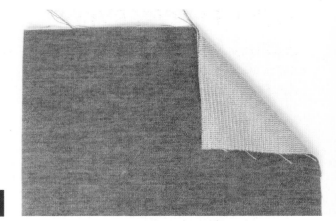

A

B

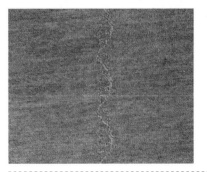

Many machines are capable of embroidering straight rows of decorative stitches.

SNAP ON

LOW SHANK

HIGH SHANK

SLANT SHANK

BERNINA

DARNING/FREE MOTION FOOT

By lowering the feed teeth (see your owner's manual), a darning or free motion foot allows you to hover above the fabric so you can move the fabric freely, stitching any sort of design. These feet come in regular free motion or spring free motion. The spring free motion provides a tiny hooping action with every stitch. If you are working on lightweight fabrics, consider applying stabilizer to the wrong side of the fabric to minimize stitch puckering.

A

1. Lower the feed teeth (feed dogs) on the sewing machine (refer to your owner's manual).

2. Set the machine for a long stitch and slow speed control.

3. Attach the presser foot by pinching the spring mechanism as you guide the foot into place, so the arm is resting above the needle clamp area. Nonspring feet are attached the same as other presser feet (A).

4. Lower the presser foot to engage the thread tension as you sew.

5. Practice stitching on scrap fabric (with stabilizer if you are going to apply stabilizer to the project fabric) to ensure the best length and width settings. Stitch slowly and move the fabric as you stitch.

6. Switch to zigzag stitches and see how the stitches look and feel.

LOW SHANK (SPRING)

LOW SHANK

HIGH SHANK (SPRING)

SLANT SHANK (SPRING)

BERNINA

How to Thread Paint

1. You can stitch freely in a random pattern. This typically is done during quilting, with padding between the fabric layers (B). Or you can mark a simple design on your fabric.

2. Set up the machine as described above and follow the design lines or stitch as desired (C).

3. This technique is not meant to be precise, so loosen up and let yourself stitch outside the lines; this adds to the freehand, artistic feel of the finished project (D).

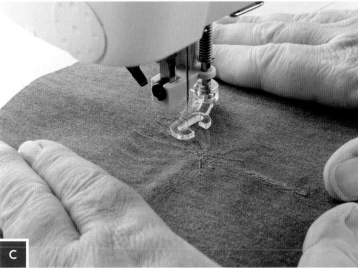

How to Attach Lace

1. Pin or baste lace to the fabric edge. You can trim away both lace and fabric edges later.

2. Set up the machine as described above. Set your machine for a straight or narrow zigzag stitch.

3. Place the fabric and lace in the stitching area and lower the presser foot. Stitch slowly in a meandering pattern to randomize your stitches or make them blend with the shapes of the lace embroidery (A).

4. Continue stitching along the design lines of the lace to finish stitching the lace to the fabric. Trim the lace from the top and the fabric from the bottom (B).

TIP: I discovered this technique when altering a wedding dress. I was shortening the skirt, which was a creamy sheer organza with lace appliqué all along the bottom edge. At first, I thought I'd have to painstakingly sew the lace back on with a straight stitch pivoting as I went along. But when I looked closer at how it was originally applied, I noticed the beautiful random meandering stitches that only come from free-motion embroidery! This method has saved me hundreds of hours since.

A

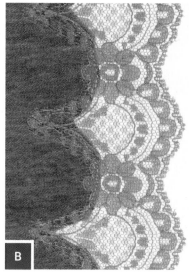

B

OPEN TOE APPLIQUÉ FOOT

Appliqué is the process of attaching one decorative or shaped layer of fabric to another. Sometimes, the decorative layer (or appliqué) is fused to the base fabric, making it easier to stitch around the edges. Stitching covers the raw edge of the appliqué fabric and prevents it from fraying. Reverse appliqué is a different technique in which you join two pieces of fabric in design patterns and then trim away the top fabric inside the stitching line. The open toe appliqué foot allows you to guide the work accurately because you can see the stitching area clearly, so you can react and adjust the stitching before you've gotten too far off the mark.

1. Prepare the base fabric with stabilizer, if needed.

2. To make the appliqué, attach fusible web to the wrong side of the appliqué fabric. Trace or draw the appliqué shape on the right side of the fabric and cut out the design/shape.

3. Peel off the paper backing from the fusible web and fuse the appliqué to the base fabric, according to the package instructions.

4. Set your machine for the satin stitch. Be sure to practice stitching on scrap fabric to determine the length and width of the zigzag to your liking. (A zigzag that's too stacked can make the project pucker a bit.)

5. Lift the presser foot, move the fabrics to the sewing area, sink the needle into the starting position at the edge of the appliqué, and lower the foot.

6. Begin stitching slowly and pause with the needle down to navigate curves and corners (A).

7. Continue stitching until you reach the beginning, overlapping by a couple of stitches.

A

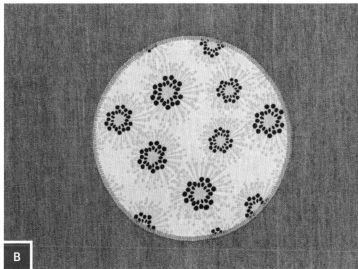

B

8. Pull the threads to the back of the work with a hand sewing needle to tie off and secure them. This allows you to keep a consistent stitch all around your design without the bulk of backstitches to indicate where you stopped and started (B).

SNAP ON

LOW SHANK

HIGH SHANK

SLANT SHANK

BERNINA

COUCHING/BRAIDING FOOT

Couching is a decorative technique that sews braid, cording, or any narrow trim to a base fabric to create a raised design. This vintage-looking technique adds a great, dramatic effect to any project. The couching/braiding foot allows you to guide the trim easily and still see stitching guidelines as you sew.

1. Prepare your fabric with stabilizer, if needed, to keep the work from puckering. Use a fabric marking pen to draw the design lines you'd like the trim to follow.

2. Set your machine for a narrow zigzag that just covers the trim on either side, so the stitches do not extend past the trim. Set the stitch length between 3 and 4, because a longer stitch length allows the stitch to travel and not cover too much of the trim. Practice on scrap fabric.

3. Insert the trim into the foot as shown. Attach the foot to the machine, leaving 1" to 2" (2.5 to 5 cm) of trim to hold as you begin stitching (A).

4. Position your fabric and the trim in the sewing area. Lower the presser foot and begin to stitch, following the marked guidelines and attaching the trim to the fabric with the stitches (B).

5. Finish attaching the trim and backstitch two or three stitches at the end.

6. Trim the ends of the threads; keep the ends from raveling with seam sealant (C).

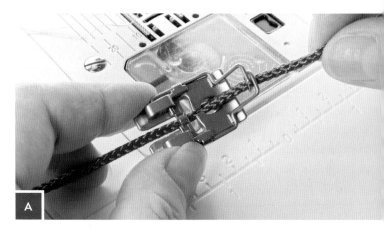

A

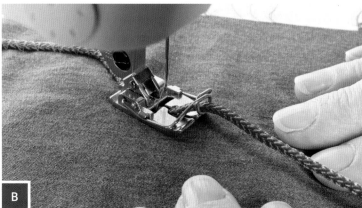

B

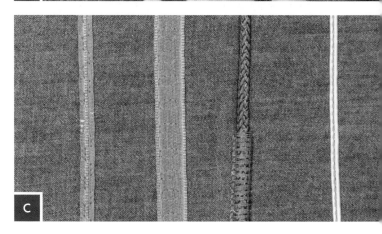

C

Use the corresponding shank adaptor for your type of machine.

TIP: Attaching the trim to wider curves is easiest, but you will master tight turns with practice. When turning tight curves or corners, stop with the needle down on the inside edge and lift the presser foot to pivot the work. Then begin sewing again; repeat as needed to finish attaching the trim.

WING NEEDLE

Wing needles might just be my favorite gadgets. They pierce fabric, and because of their wing shape, they pry an opening between the woven fibers. The stitch you use determines how the hole stays open. If you love the hemstitching detail on vintage linens, invest in wing needles. You can use a regular needle with the hemstitch, but it doesn't produce the open work as much as a wing needle does. The hemstitching and wing needle combination works best with lightweight woven fabrics, such as linen, or lightweight cotton, such as organdy or batiste.

Explore all the different looks you can achieve with the wing needle and other stitches. They work best on stitches that are symmetrical and have a simple repeat. They don't work well with irregular decorative embroidery designs like vines or leaves.

1. Starch and press your fabric.

2. Set your machine for a hemstitch. (If your machine doesn't have a hemstitch, you can use a zigzag stitch.) Practice stitching on scrap fabric to determine the best stitch length and width settings. You will also want to practice with higher needle tension settings to create more open holes (A).

3. Stitch the first row, slowly making sure the tension is a bit high to create wider holes (B).

4. Place the hemstitching row you just stitched back under the sewing area and let the needle sink into one of the previous holes on the right side of the first row of stitches. Now you can continue sewing and the machine will track into the same holes, creating a design that's double the first one (C).

BRIDGING GUIDES

One of the coolest things I've learned to do on the sewing machine is to join two fabrics with decorative stitches. It evokes the painstaking, delicate handwork you see on vintage textiles of all kinds. You will find this type of stitching on women's blouses, heirloom baby apparel, and home décor. I love it because it looks complex and beautiful.

The low-tech, how-to version of this technique is to secure a bridging guide to the area in front of your needle that allows you to guide two pieces of fabric or trim into the sewing area while maintaining an even distance. A wide decorative stitch then joins the two pieces and "sews" in midair where there's no fabric, creating a delicate thread design between the two pieces.

1. Set your machine for a wide decorative stitch that's symmetrical and fairly simple.

2. Measure the width of the stitch to determine the best bridging guide. Install the bridging guide so that the sloped area on the guide is furthest from the needle (the slope accommodates the curve of the presser foot).

3. Practice stitching using two pieces of scrap fabric.

4. Prepare the fabric by applying fusible interfacing to the wrong side, if the fabric is lightweight, or apply spray starch. Press a straight fold along each fabric edge that will be joined by the stitches (A).

5. Guide the two folded edges of the fabric pieces along each side of the bridging guide and lower the presser foot to hold the pieces in place. Start stitching, holding the work from the front with your right hand and the thread tails with your left hand (B). Stitch slowly for better control.

6. A basic bridging stitch, plus zigzag, feather, and cross stitches used as bridging stitches (C).

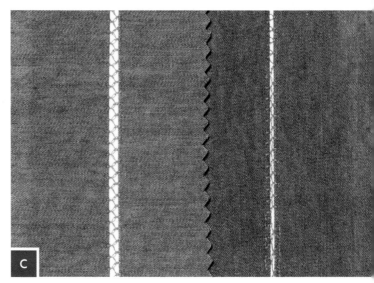

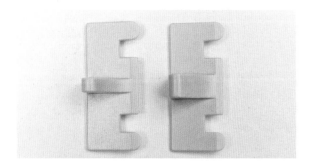

PINTUCK FOOT

If you've ever tried to stitch perfectly parallel rows of tiny tucks, you know it's more difficult than standard tucks. The pintuck foot helps you guide narrow rows of fabric with a series of tiny slots on the underside of the foot. You can also use a twin needle to speed the process.

1. Set your machine for a straight stitch and tighten the tension a bit. You might want to make a practice pintuck on scrap fabric.

2. Stitch the first pintuck, making it as straight as you can.

3. To finish the first pintuck, make a single backstitch and trim your threads.

4. Starting back at the top of the fabric, align the first tuck under the groove in the pintuck foot that is two away from the center groove.

5. Stitch the second pintuck slowly, making sure the first tuck stays in the groove under the foot (A).

6. Continue until you have stitched the desired number of pintucks (B).

SNAP ON

LOW SHANK

HIGH SHANK

SLANT SHANK

BERNINA

FRINGE FOOT

The fringe foot is also called a joining foot. To create fringe, you only need to stitch on a single layer of fabric to create a thick layer of arching upper stitches.

1. For light- to medium-weight fabrics, it is a good idea to use stabilizer (see page 36).

2. Use a fabric marking pen to draw the design lines you wish to follow or a specific design that will work with the fringe effect.

3. Thread your machine with contrasting-color bobbin thread.

4. Set your machine for the satin stitch, with a short stitch length and wide stitch width. Practice stitching on scrap fabric.

Using the Fringe Foot as a Joining Foot

The fringe/joining foot can be used to join two pieces of fabric that abut, with no space between them. Simply set your machine for a zigzag stitch and position the metal guide on the presser foot between the fabrics as you stitch. After stitching, wiggle the fabric pieces back and forth to equalize the upper and lower threads, creating the appearance of a faggoting stitch.

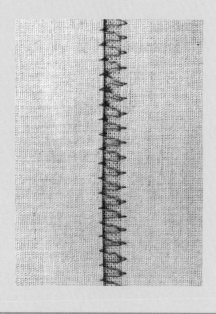

SNAP ON

LOW SHANK

HIGH SHANK

SLANT SHANK

BERNINA

5. Stitch along the marked design lines.

6. Press the thread loops to one side (this will make a row of stitching on the side you're pressing away from visible).

7. Change to a straight stitch with a length of 1.5.

8. Sew along the flattened edge, just inside the loops. Backstitch at the beginning and end (A).

9. On the back of the fabric, identify the bobbin thread. Use a seam ripper to remove the bobbin thread.

10. When the bobbin thread is gone, use the seam ripper to gently pull the threads to the front of the fabric, creating the fringe (B).

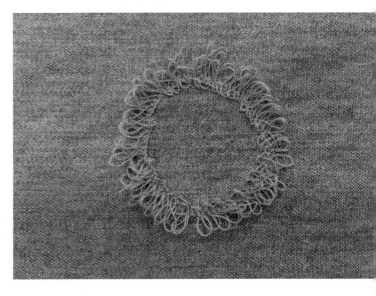

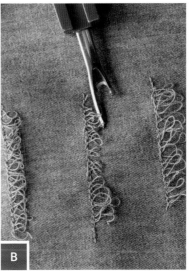

LACE APPLIQUÉ DRESS REFASHION

Trends come and go, and most fashion trends seem to come back around, eventually, but in slightly different ways. Lace adds dimension and texture to fabric and is a quick and easy way to update an older garment. You can add pieces of lace with the free motion foot (see page 118), but you can also apply the lace with a straight stitch and then cut away the backing, as shown in this classic shirtdress.

If you have a favorite shirt or dress in the back of your closet or find a dress in your local thrift shop that just needs a bit of updating, simply insert lace trim for a completely new look. Plan your design before you purchase the lace so you can determine exactly how much lace you need. Be sure to wash and press the garment before you start planning your update!

Finished size: Varies

Stitch type: Straight stitch, optional hemstitch

Length: Straight stitch: 2.5, Hemstitch: test for best results

Width: Straight stitch: 0, Hemstitch: test for best results

MATERIALS

Garment that needs updating

Lace trim, enough to complete design

Spray starch

All-purpose thread

Fabric marking pen

Pins

Fabric shears

ACCESSORIES

Straight stitch plate

Straight stitch foot

Free motion foot (optional)

Universal needle

Wing needle (if hemstitching is desired)

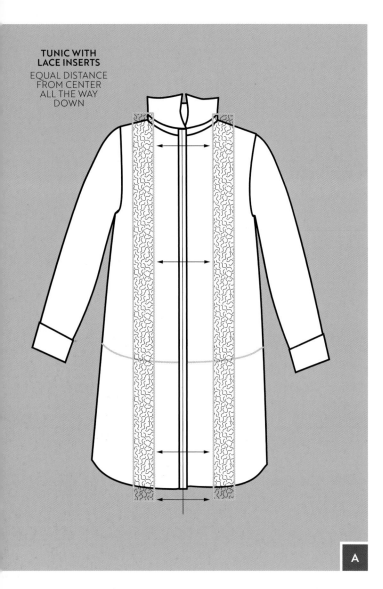

TUNIC WITH LACE INSERTS

EQUAL DISTANCE
FROM CENTER
ALL THE WAY
DOWN

A

UPDATING THE DRESS

1. Preshrink the lace if it is 100 percent cotton by submerging it in hot water and hanging it to dry.

2. Apply starch to the wrong side of the garment in the area you will appliquéing.

3. Use a fabric pen to mark guidelines or design lines on the garment for where you plan to apply the lace. The lines should be evenly spaced from the visual center of the garment. In this case, it's the buttons and buttonholes (A).

4. Pin the lace to the garment along the guidelines. Allow about ½" (1.3 cm) of lace to extend beyond the garment at the top and bottom edges for hemming (B).

5. If the lace trim has one or both straight edges, use the straight stitch plate and foot to stitch just on top of the straight edges. If the lace trim has one or both shaped edges, use the free motion foot as on page 118. The lace in the example has one straight and one shaped edge.

6. Turn the garment wrong side out. Carefully cut up the entire length of the garment behind the lace. Clip diagonally into the corners at the top of the garment so you can clean finish the raw edges.

7. If you straight stitched the lace in place, trim away the fabric, leaving ¼" (6 mm) seam allowance on both sides of the lace. Press the seam allowance ¼" (6 mm) to the wrong side and straight stitch or hemstitch through all the layers. This makes a clean finish on the inside. If you used the free motion foot to secure the lace, simply trim away the extra fabric, following the shape of the stitches.

8. Turn the raw edges of the lace at the neckline ¼" (6 mm) to the wrong side and topstitch.

9. To hem the lace on the bottom of the garment, fold the lace ¼" (6 mm) to the wrong side (or to follow the shape of hemline) and topstitch.

Use the pintuck foot to add several rows of tucks, or create multiple rows of hemstitching now that you know how to use these feet!

MONOGRAMMED PILLOW WITH FREE MOTION THREAD PAINTING

Pillows are some of the easiest projects to make and are a great way to practice new skills and use techniques that might be too difficult in a bigger project. This chalkboard-inspired pillow lets you dip your toe into the world of free motion embroidery and makes a cute gift, as well.

Finished size: 18" × 18" (45 × 45 cm)

Stitch type: Straight stitch

Length: 5

Width: 0

MATERIALS

¾ yd (.68 m) fabric

¾ yd (.68 m) fusible interfacing

Rayon embroidery thread

14" (35.6 cm) invisible zipper

All-purpose thread

18" × 18" (45 × 45 cm) pillow form and/or polyester fiberfill

Fabric shears

Ironing board

Iron

Wax chalk or a water-soluble marker

Pins

Measuring tape

ACCESSORIES

Universal/zigzag foot

Free motion foot

Invisible zipper foot

Standard zipper foot

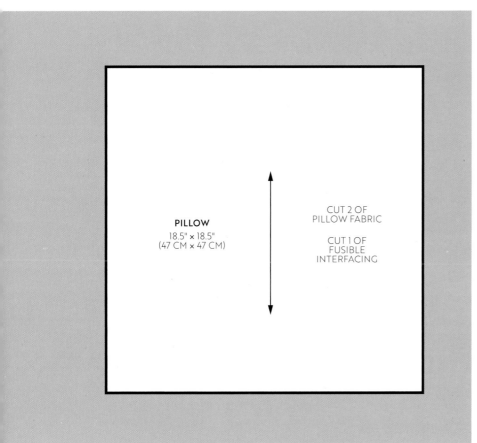

PILLOW
18.5" × 18.5"
(47 CM × 47 CM)

CUT 2 OF
PILLOW FABRIC

CUT 1 OF
FUSIBLE
INTERFACING

CUTTING AND PREPARING THE FABRIC

See cutting diagram on left.

1. Cut 2 pieces of pillow fabric and 1 piece of fusible interfacing 18½" × 18½" (47 × 47 cm).

2. Fuse the interfacing to the wrong side of one of the fabric pieces, following the package instructions. This fabric piece will be the pillow front.

A

THREAD PAINTING THE PILLOW FRONT

1. Mark the design on the pillow front with wax chalk or a water-soluble marker (A).

2. Use rayon embroidery thread for the needle and the bobbin thread. Set your sewing machine for a straight stitch with a 4 or 5 length. Install the free motion foot.

3. Set the speed control to slow and stitch several samples to refine the stitch settings and speed control until you feel confident.

4. Begin thread painting the design, working in small areas. Keep your motions fluid, knowing you can restitch anything that's amiss. Keep the stitches sketchy and light, and fill them in later, as needed, to emphasize with more coverage (B).

5. For this chalkboard style embroidery font, group stitches together so you can see them from a distance, leaving open negative space for that chalky, sketched-in look (C).

TIP: You can also use an embroidery hoop to keep your project smooth and even. Use a hoop that will fit into the sewing area and allow free movement. For ease of movement on the underside of the moving fabric, you can find add-on accessories for your machine, such as Teflon mats made to help the free motion project glide freely around the sewing area.

B

C

MAKING THE PILLOW

Unless otherwise noted, all seam allowances are ½" (1.3 cm).

1. Install the invisible zipper foot centered along one edge of the pillow. Rethread the machine with all-purpose thread. Refer to chapter 3, page 66 for how to apply an invisible zipper (D).

2. Change to a standard zipper foot to finish the seams at the beginning and end of the zipper.

3. With right sides together and the zipper slightly open, stitch the front and back pillow pieces together around the remaining three sides.

4. Trim the corners diagonally and press open the seams (E).

5. At each corner, pin the side seams to the bottom/top seams to form boxed corners as in the Pencil Pouch project (page 53).

6. Measure 1" (2.5 cm) from each corner and mark a horizontal line across the point at the 1" (2.5 cm) mark.

7. Stitch along the horizontal line, backstitching at the beginning and end of the seam. Trim and press open the seam (F).

8. Turn the pillow cover right side out through the zipper and insert the pillow form, filling the corners with polyester fiberfill. Or simply stuff the entire pillow cover with polyfill. Zip the pillowcase closed.

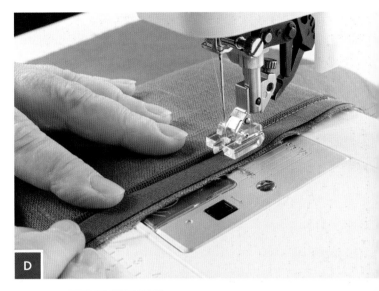

D

E

F

LINEN NAPKINS WITH DECORATIVE STITCHING

Linen napkins with contrast hemstitching will never go out of style. Make as many as you want—it will be great practice mitering corners and perfecting decorative stitching.

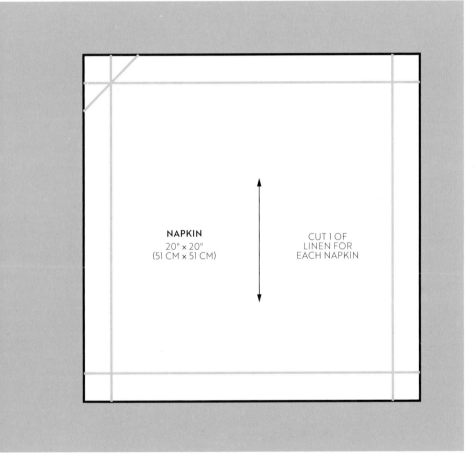

NAPKIN
20" × 20"
(51 CM × 51 CM)

CUT 1 OF
LINEN FOR
EACH NAPKIN

Finished size: 17" × 17" (43.2 cm × 43.2 cm)

Stitch type: Straight stitch and hem stitch

Length: 2.5 for straight stitch, Hem stitch: test for best results

Width: 0 for straight stitch, Hem stitch: test for best results

MATERIALS FOR 6 NAPKINS

2 yd (1.8 m) linen

All-purpose thread

Rayon embroidery thread

Spray starch or sizing (optional)

Ironing board

Iron

Ruler

Fabric shears

Fabric marker

Pins

ACCESSORIES

Universal/zigzag foot

Universal needle

Wing needle

CUTTING THE FABRIC

See cutting diagram on left.

1. Prewash and press the fabric.
2. Measure and cut 6 squares, each 20" × 20" (51 × 51 cm) or whatever size napkins you prefer.

A

MAKING THE NAPKINS

1. Use a fabric marker and ruler to mark 1½" (3.8 cm) from each edge on the wrong side of the fabric. Then draw a 45-degree line across each corner, intersecting the two previous lines (A).

2. With right sides together and at each corner, pin the diagonal lines together, backstitching at the beginning and end. Trim the seam allowance and across the corner. Press the seam open (B).

3. Turn the napkin right side out and press (C).

4. Machine baste around the raw edges.

5. Make a tiny dot with a pencil or water-soluble marker at the point where the decorative stitching will meet at each corner, 1" (2.5 cm) from each side.

B

C

6. Make a bobbin, and thread the needle with rayon embroidery thread, set your machine for a hemstitch, and insert a wing needle.

7. Hemstitch 1" (2.5 cm) from the finished edges, pivoting 90 degrees, with the needle down, at each corner. Slow down and use the hand wheel to approach the corner, and make sure you stop on the marked dot with the needle down and on the outside of the stitch pattern (D).

8. Sew the remaining sides and overlap one small area of stitching when you reach the beginning (E).

9. Remove the basting threads and trim the raw edges close to the hemstitch, taking care not to clip the hemstitch threads.

10. Press; apply starch or sizing to get a smooth, crisp finish, if desired.

D

E

GLOSSARY

Awl: A hand tool with a sharp tip used to make a hole in something or push something that can't be held with fingers.

Baste: To sew loosely, with a large running stitch, to secure pieces together or mark something temporarily.

Bias: The direction of fabric that's on a 45-degree angle from straight of grain.

Bobbin: Small spool that holds thread under the throat plate of the machine.

Cover plate: Plate that covers feed teeth, has a hole for the needle to go through, and has guidelines to help you stitch straight.

Disappearing ink fabric marker: A marker with colored ink that disappears after time or when wiped with water.

Felt pad: A small pad around the base of the spool pin.

Gather: To compress a length of fabric into a smaller length so the fabric forms small, irregular pleats on both sides of the stitching line.

Gridded ruler: A clear plastic ruler with a grid printed on it.

Hem: To create a finished edge on the bottom of a garment or sleeve.

Interfacing: A layer of fabric, applied to the wrong side of a piece of fabric, to stabilize it, add weight, or make it less transparent.

Knit: A type of fabric that is formed by looping fibers together in a knitting process.

Lightweight fusible tricot interfacing: A very light nylon knit fusible interfacing preferred by contemporary manufacturing for its universal applications. Some entire garments are bonded with this to give lightweight fashion fabric more body.

Machine baste: To make a basting stitch using a sewing machine, usually set for the longest stitch.

Miter: To make a seam at a diagonal angle to join two hems that intersect at a corner.

Needle: The needle delivers the thread down between the fibers of the fabric to intersect with the bobbin thread.

Needle bar: A vertical post to which the needle is mounted.

Needle clamp: The clamp that holds the needle on the needle bar.

Needle clamp screw: The screw that tightens or loosens the needle clamp.

Overlock: A type of stitch that loops around to finish raw edges of a piece of fabric, also a machine that makes this stitch while trimming the edge of the fabric.

Pleat: A fold of fabric that adds fullness to a garment.

Press open: To press open a stitched seam using an iron, creating a more finished exterior seam line.

Presser bar: A vertical post to which presser feet mount.

Rolled hem: A very tiny hem that can be done either by machine or by hand, often seen on the edge of delicate fabrics. The fabric rolls over the raw edge and is secured with a delicate row of topstitching.

Ruching: Another term for gathers, made by pulling a long, running stitch that has been made across the width of a piece of fabric.

Seam allowance: The area between the raw edge of the fabric and the stitch.

Seam ripper: A pointed, handheld tool used to remove stitches.

Spool cap: A cap that holds the spool on the spool pin and keeps thread from catching on the edges of the spool.

Spool pin: The spool pin holds the thread, sometimes vertically, sometimes horizontally.

Staystitching: A row of stitching used to stabilize an area that is likely to stretch during the handling process, such as a neckline or an arm hole, but can be used anywhere stability is needed.

Stitch plate: *See* cover plate.

Straight stitch plate: Cover plate with a small needle hole.

Tailor's chalk: A chalky or waxy marking tool that comes off after the garment is sewn.

Take-up lever: A lever that maintains tension on the thread as it feeds into the needle.

Tension disks: The tension disks regulate the speed that the thread feeds into the needle.

Thread baste: To loosely sew two layers together temporarily, instead of using pins.

Thread guides: Thread guides keep the thread from snagging on something.

Thread path: Threading direction.

Throat plate: *See* Cover plate.

Topstitching: A row of stitching that usually runs parallel to the edge of a garment.

Twill tape: A woven ribbon with a twill weave pattern. It is usually made of cotton, in black or white, and is available in multiple widths.

Wonder under: Fusible bonding web for fusing two fabrics together.

Woven: Fabric manufactured by weaving threads together using a loom.

Zigzag: A stitch that goes from right to left, creating small points on either side.

ACKNOWLEDGMENTS

Thanks to Joy Aquilino, Beth Baumgartel, Heather Godin, Timothy Hughes, Tarah Hiemes, Meredith Quinn, Lisa Trudeau, Jane Glenn, Tricia Waddell, Jen Mulder, Margaret Jankowski, Bari J. Ackerman, Jay Mulder, The Electric Needle, The Sewing Machine Project, Trish Pulvermacher, Mario Gahona, Monetti Tailoring, Costume People Facebook Group, Mary Devitt, Deb Griffith, and Marn Sandum for your knowledge and generosity.

Thanks to Lane, Tess, and David Lincecum for your love and support, and to my Sewing Machine Feet from A to Z Craftsy class for your questions and insights.

ABOUT THE AUTHOR

Steffani Lincecum is the author of *Patternmaking for a Perfect Fit* (Potter Craft, 2010) and teaches about sewing online for Craftsy.com. She's been creating for theater, film, and television since 1985 and currently lives in Wisconsin, where she writes and works with American Players Theater, Forward Theatre Co., and the Children's Theatre of Madison as a draper, designer, and teaching artist. Her online sewing community is at Stitchcoach.com.

INDEX